KU-547-160

THE VOGUE FACTOR

KIRSTIE CLEMENTS

gff

CONTENTS

MAY 2012: REGIME CHANGE

It was 10 a.m. on a Wednesday. I had a scheduled meeting with Nicole Sheffield, the newly appointed CEO of NewsLifeMedia, the company owned by Rupert Murdoch that had held the licence for *Vogue* in Australia since 2007. We had met only once before, a quick and pleasant chat in her office in March a few weeks after she had started.

I had been working at *Vogue Australia* for twenty-five years and in the editor's chair for thirteen. She was my eighth CEO. Magazines were going through a tough time in the face of a digital onslaught, but *Vogue* was faring better than others. Circulation was steady, subscriptions and readership were at an all-time high, we reached our advertising targets each month and held the greater market share. We had also been voted Magazine of the Year the previous November at the annual Australian Magazine Awards, and were commended by industry leaders for our consistent excellence, innovation and quality. Given that

Nicole had less experience in luxury publishing, in particular *Vogue*, I anticipated she would value my input.

I took the lift up to the second floor without any inkling of what was about to happen. Her PA looked jumpy.

'Hi, I'm here for my meeting with Nicole,' I said cheerily.

'Yes, they're in there,' she said, pointing towards a usually unoccupied office, quite clearly not Nicole's. Something was up.

The realisation began to dawn. It dripped down from my head to my toes in slow motion, as if treacle had been poured over me. I walked in and saw the human resources director sitting at the table with a folder and a jug of water, one of those cheap ones pretending to be a Georg Jensen. The presence of HR always meant bad news. Nicole was shifting in her chair, shooting longing glances at the open door—clearly in a hurry to do what she had come here for. I knew exactly what was going to happen.

'You're kidding,' I said calmly.

'I'm sure this is a shock, but I just think we need new leadership,' Nicole said in rapid-fire. 'Condé Nast are in full support of this.' Condé Nast International is the parent company of *Vogue Australia*, and an organisation I had developed a strong relationship with over the years. Nicole repeated that Condé Nast knew all about it, probably thinking I was going to put up a protest and try to get the chairman, Jonathan Newhouse, on speed dial.

But for some reason I felt strangely relieved. There had been increasing pressure on the brand, with reduced budgets and pages, and the retrenching of crucial editorial staff. The holy mantra was 'digital' and we had been waiting endlessly for funding to progress and evolve, but it felt as if the magazine itself was regarded as a burden. No one wanted to listen to my views on the importance of maintaining quality or protecting the brand. Not even Condé Nast. I was however, stunned by their lack of loyalty. Obviously their main interest was the licensing cheques.

I decided not to let a wonderful, stimulating quarter-century at *Vogue* be diminished. How you conduct yourself on the way out is more important than how you went in. It didn't occur to me to ask who the new 'leader' would be. I really didn't care. Nicole had at this point left the room anyway, and I was faced with a scarlet-faced HR director who instructed me to leave the building immediately without speaking to my team—my amazing and loyal colleagues, some of whom I had worked with for more than thirteen years, and many of whom would also be shown the door shortly afterwards.

The whole episode was devoid of any graciousness, and perfectly reflective of a new mood in publishing. As I picked up my handbag and walked out the door, I turned my phone on silent and braced myself for the media who would swoop like vultures.

The *Vogue* I knew was over.

1

NOT YOUR AVERAGE DESK JOB

I had two priorities after I finished my Higher School Certificate. One was to get out of the Sutherland Shire, the conservative, soporific area south of Sydney where I grew up. Two was to write.

My civil engineer father Joseph passed away when I was five, and my mother Gloria had worked two jobs to raise me and my older brother Anthony. I certainly wasn't going to blame her for the sexist, surfie mentality of the Shire, but I knew by the age of thirteen that being literally barked at by morons outside the North Cronulla pub was not going to be my future. The barking meant you were a dog—because you were a brunette, pale skinned, a bit chubby or wearing the wrong swimsuit. I chose to see it as a badge of honour, because they didn't do it to the resident high school bully Karen, who was blonde, pretty, tanned, and had the IQ of a platform wedge.

I found the conformity stifling, and so decided that I should move to what appeared to be the least conformist suburb in Sydney: Kings Cross. In 1979 I broke the news to my mother at the age of seventeen that I was going to move into my own apartment. Although she had reservations about the seedy neighbourhood I had chosen, Mum knew I could take care of myself. She didn't feel the same way I did about the Shire. Having grown up in post-World War II Paddington, in her opinion she had escaped the harrowing inner-city slums by moving to the bright and shiny outer suburb of verdant Sylvania. My adventurous streak told me that travel, rather than university was what I needed, so I set my sights on getting out of there as soon as I could.

I applied for a job advertised in the newspaper and became a stockbroking clerk. It was a boom time for the market, and a number of lucrative bonuses enabled me to travel Europe for one year at the age of eighteen, then again at twenty-one. No backpacks—I would like to clarify that straight away. No hippie stuff. Always a suitcase. And always in full makeup.

I wrote constantly when on the road, short stories just for myself; in hotel rooms in Rome, on trains to Berlin, in hostels in Athens and bedsits in London. I travelled until the money ran out.

By 1985 I had returned to Sydney and was working as a sales assistant at an arty bookshop. My boyfriend at the time was running the Chauvel Cinema in Paddington, so I would leave work in the afternoon and join him in the evening, selling tickets or running the bar. It was an exciting, formative period. I read books all day and saw almost every important film ever made at night. I became immersed in French Nouvelle Vague, Japanese porn, film noir, Visconti and Fassbinder. Actors such as Judy Davis would come into the store to buy poetry and plays.

But I was twenty-three, and dusting the books was getting up my nose. One day during my lunch break, I scanned the Jobs Vacant section of the *Sydney Morning Herald* and there was a tiny advertisement. 'Receptionist wanted at *Vogue*.'

'Imagine,' I thought to myself. 'Imagine the world that would open up!'

I rang the number numerous times until—bingo—I scored a rendezvous. As I could not leave the bookstore until 5 p.m., I was to be the last candidate interviewed the next day, at 6 p.m. I rushed home after work to shower, put on the best dress I owned and a pair of pink ballet slippers, and took a taxi I couldn't afford to make sure I would be right on time.

Vogue at that time was housed in a charming older building in Clarence Street, Sydney, spread across a number of floors, all serviced by a clanking elevator operated by a driver called Col. I sat down for my interview with a woman named Norma Mary Marshall. She was probably in her mid-sixties and absolutely stunning. She had bright-blue eyes, an elegant puff of white-blonde hair and a knockout pair of legs. She'd worked at *Vogue* forever and was—I discovered later—quite the party girl. I never knew what her exact role was, but it might as well have been something like 'glamorous ambassador'. She was sipping from a bone-china teacup that I'm pretty sure was filled with gin. I liked her on sight.

Norma Mary asked me if I had ever worked a switchboard. I lied and said, 'Of course'.

'Well, I've seen twenty girls, and you're the last but you're the prettiest,' she said, and we laughed. 'But I've already decided on someone else, so I think I'll put her on for a week and then you for a week, for a trial.'

I don't know what made me say it, as I was terribly nervous, but I replied: 'Why don't you put me on first? If I work out, then I can just stay and it will save you the trouble.' I was in.

A week or so later I was sitting at the *Vogue* reception desk. I hadn't been able to sleep the night before from nerves and excitement. It appeared that absolutely every individual who worked in the building was fabulous. Nobody *walked* past my desk, they swept past, jackets flung over shoulders, silk scarves flying out behind. Everyone was always in a very dramatic and stylish rush to be somewhere else.

The editor-in-chief at the time was June McCallum, who was feared and revered. Fiercely intelligent and equally impatient, June was famous for getting straight to the point. She had spent many years working as a journalist in London and had a view on far more than just fashion. She also had a closed-door policy, and people would wait nervously for days for an appointment to see her. The only contact I had with June for my first six months at *Vogue* was to catch a glimpse of her through the glass, swishing past on her way to the lift, a formidable brunette with her signature wooden bangles rattling loudly.

The fashion office was on the ground floor, to the right of reception, and that was where all the action happened. I had managed to master the very basic switchboard in about five minutes on Day One, so I was sitting excitedly at the desk, anticipating all kinds of wild and improbable happenings, when an incredibly handsome young man walked in and handed me his modelling portfolio. And then another. And then another. Soon the area had filled up with gorgeous male specimens, who sat casually on the seagrass-matting floor making small talk between themselves, as well as to me, when the chairs had run out. Day One and, as luck would have it, it was male model casting day.

Then came the delivery of all the latest international fashion magazines, to be handed out to staff later. I could read any or all of them. Clothes were being constantly delivered by couriers and *Vogue* staff members kept darting by, shooting me dazzling, friendly smiles.

The beauty editor Karin Upton sauntered past at one point, wearing a Claude Montana raincoat with stupendous eighties shoulder pads and a tiny short-skirted Chanel suit. 'Karin, did you get your hair cut while you were away?' asked Judith Cook, the fashion director, who was in reception to collect a model's portfolio.

'No, no, I would never let anyone in New York touch my hair!' replied Karin.

I decided then and there I was never going to leave.

* * *

The managing director of Condé Nast was (surprisingly forward-thinking for those times) a woman, Eve Harman. Tall and elegant, with high cheekbones and a silvery-blonde bob, Eve had the most beautiful diction, smoked cigarettes and called everyone 'darling'. I was in awe of her. Then again, I was in awe of almost everyone.

The *Vogue* women in those years were in a league of their own. Their style was not just related to fashion, or which designer was hot or not. They lived and breathed *Vogue*, their taste extending through to their homes, their art, their dinner parties, their holidays. There was Marion von Adlerstein, the travel editor, whippet-thin with her crisp white shirts, skinny black pants, silver cropped hair and long cigarellos. Judith Cook, the ultra-chic fashion director, whose interest in art, literature and film informed all her fashion choices. Nancy Pilcher, the executive editor who originally hailed from the US, with her tiny waist, thick, long, blonde hair, and her incredible Sante Fe/Ralph Lauren style. Carolyn 'Charlie' Lockhart, the editor of the groundbreaking *Vogue Entertaining Guide*: again, in a class all of her own. I had been transported to a world of infinite taste, mentored by women who were neither snobbish nor judgemental. They were warm, intelligent and wickedly funny.

As good as the reception desk was, it had its quiet moments, and I began to look for other things to do. I noticed that the fashion stockroom needed tidying. Note to any future interns reading this book: fashion stockrooms always need tidying. As I was on good terms with all the girls in the fashion office, I thought I may as well offer my services. I approached Judith and timidly asked if I could reorganise the drawers containing the stockings and socks. My request was met with gratitude. So I began to ask for more and more things I could do and more ways I could be helpful. I wanted to be busy, but I also wanted to know more about *Vogue*.

Nancy had just returned from the international shows, so I suggested that I type up her notes for her. And could I help pack suitcases for the shoots? Also, did Karin need help to rearrange the beauty cupboard? Without really thinking too much about it I began to make myself more and more useful. Then one day, as Nancy rushed past, I decided to push my luck. 'Nancy, if by any chance you are ever looking for an assistant, could I ask that you consider me?' I had developed a bit of a girl crush on Nancy. She is one of those people who lights up a room.

And so she made it happen. Coincidentally, there was a position open for an assistant in *Vogue* promotions. This is the department in a magazine that produces advertising pages for clients, which have an editorial look and feel. I was offered the job, on the proviso that I would also assist Nancy. Not even six months since I had started and I was off the reception desk.

Promotions was a brilliant training ground because you worked on every detail of a job, from conceptualising the shoot, casting the models, and choosing the clothes, the photographer and the location. Naturally I put my hand up for every task. Could I write the captions? Could I also try writing the headings? In promotions, you also learned to manage client expectations, while trying to maintain artistic integrity. It was an invaluable introduction to magazine politics and the inevitable dance between commerce and creativity.

It was then I began to understand the level of perfectionism expected at *Vogue*. It was extraordinary. Corners were never, and I mean *never*, to be cut. The dress, the tablecloth, the heading all had to be just so. It was all very *Madame Bovary*. Nothing was ever good enough. A philosophy that could drive you mad or spur you to do better. I chose the latter.

For one job, we were to shoot an image for Schiaparelli hosiery that required a good pair of legs and some shoes. I called in dozens and dozens of shoes for Nancy to choose from. She settled on one pair she liked. I then proceeded to set up a model casting, just for legs. Models can have particular attributes that they specialise in—hand models, foot models, models who can smile. We spent all day asking dozens of girls from four different agencies to parade around the creative services office and show us their legs, until finally Nancy said: 'No, none of these are right.' Keeping in mind we only required the legs, not the top half. My mind was reeling at the thought that one day I was going to have to find a *whole* model who passed the *Vogue* test, top to bottom.

The shoot was the next day. The photographer had been booked. Time was ticking. I paced the office in a panic and then collapsed dramatically across the desk of the art assistant Fiona. I looked down and noticed something I already knew. She had really fantastic legs.

The next day Fiona, the photographer Monty Coles and I were outside on Clarence Street taking the shot. These days you have to pay the council to shoot absolutely anywhere but back then you just chose a spot and took the risk. Monty strode purposefully up and down the street numerous times until he found the exact place he wanted Fiona to stand. There also happened to be a great, huge wad of chewing gum that had dried rock hard on the pavement right there. 'Can you get that off?' he said to me. Retouching was rare during that period, reserved mostly for covers or beauty shots. 'And hurry, because we are losing light,' he added. As I began to frantically scrape the gum with my fingernails, I naively asked Monty if maybe he could move to another, less gummy part of the street. It was then I learnt my first lesson about photographers, one that stayed true for the next twenty-five years. They will never, ever, do anything the easy way.

Vogue promotions carried some major accounts in those years, including regular shoots for fashion clients such as Weiss (a young and upcoming actress named Nicole Kidman featured in one advertorial) and the Australian Wool Corporation. None of it felt like work to me, it was all so varied. A huge highlight was the Bicentennial Wool Collection Fashion in 1988, where various international designers such as Claude Montana and Sonia Rykiel joined forces with local Australian designers to stage a huge fashion show at the Sydney Opera House, televised live and featuring Nancy with legendary British interviewer Michael Parkinson. My job on the night was to walk behind HRH The Princess of Wales as she mounted the steps to the concert hall. It was another pinch-me moment for someone who had just stepped away from the reception desk.

The fun really started when it was decided that Nancy and I would produce a twice-yearly supplement, called *Vogue Men*, to be attached to the back of *Vogue*. This meant producing editorial, which to me was the pinnacle. You had an entirely blank slate, forty-eight-plus empty pages ready to be brainstormed and produced. Total artistic licence. This is the core of magazine publishing and—right up until the day I left—was always the part of the job that thrilled me the most. It is also now the aspect of magazine publishing that is most under threat from commercial pressures.

Because we would be producing editorial I began to join in on general meetings, terrifying as they were. June would sit at the table, tapping her perfectly manicured blood-red fingernails on the desk if anybody stayed on one point for too long. I kept quiet for many months, just soaking it all in. I would volunteer to stack the slides from the ready-to-wear (RTW) shows into the carousel so I had something useful to do. They were then projected on the wall, and the machine would jam umpteen times while Judith and Nancy discussed which shows they had seen in Paris and Milan, what they liked, and what stories for the magazine would stem from them.

A fashion 'story' is a sequence of photographs based around a specific theme, such as denim, or tailoring, or floral dresses. This was the greatest editorial training I would ever have, and those lessons carried me through my entire career at *Vogue*. These women knew what they were talking about. They had intrinsic good taste but they also possessed cultural references. They knew the history of a designer, and why a particular show was a standout, or a disappointment. They could articulate the reason because they had the language to do so. So much amateur fashion commentary today is subjective: 'Oh, I loved the green dress, I'd wear that. The shoes are amazing!' A lot of so-called experts are merely airing fatuous personal opinions.

I recall Judith planning some fashion shoots for a particular issue, inspired by Hemingway heroines. 'We are going to approach the issue by doing two main shoots,' Judith told June during a meeting. 'The philosophy for the first one is about women who row. The other is women who are rowed.' The fashion editors literally wrote philosophies about what they were going to shoot, and why. These essays were then passed to everyone on staff—art department, sub-editors and copywriters—so that we all had an understanding about what was being featured.

There was context around things. If the shoot was to be in Africa we were encouraged to read Isak Dinesen, Marrakech, Paul Bowles. One Hemingway novel suggestion I remember for a particular shoot was *A Moveable Feast*. I ate all the literary references up. Later on, when I became fashion writer, I would spend hours with Judith in her office making up stories about shoots, wondering what a fifties-glamour girl in the Suez Canal would wear ('a shirtwaister and some leather sandals!') or the cultural implications of a safari suit. The person who would benefit most from this thoroughness was the reader. I still get cross when I look at fashion pages that have simply grouped items together because they're the same colour. Everything needs to be there for good reason. Your role as an editor is to inspire and inform, not merely collate.

Vogue Men was a great opportunity for me and I gained experience, fast. Nancy and I worked like demons, shooting all the fashion, mostly on models, but also photographing 'real' men. That's what the industry calls individuals who are not professional models: 'real people'. You very quickly become familiar with the look you're going to get from a hardcore fashion stylist when you suggest something should be shot on a 'real person', and it's not thrilled to pieces, that's for sure.

I wrote as much of *Vogue Men* as Nancy would allow, which was a great deal as our commissioning budgets were tight. This included writing all the fashion copy, cover lines, interviews with designers and popular identities—anything and everything. I was still promotions assistant, Nancy's personal assistant, and at night I covered the social functions and took names of the guests for the photographer. That was how I first met renowned social snapper Robert Rosen, whose candid photographs of the in-crowd would continue to feature in the pages of *Vogue Australia* for another twenty-five years.

The pace was intense, especially considering there were none of those fancy time-saving devices like computers or mobile phones. We posted courier bags filled with letters to the international *Vogue* offices in the afternoons, and sent telexes. The typewriters were basic. Liquid paper and carbon sheets were a necessity. In 1986 the first fax machine duly arrived, and it became one of my daily tasks to send faxes. The machine was placed upstairs with the typesetters, a group which included one particular miscreant who would regularly ask me to take off my top while I waited the agonising one and a half hours for one page to stop/start its way through. It was easy enough to just flip through a magazine and ignore him, but the mere sound of a fax machine now takes me straight back to that prehistoric cave.

But drudge work was fine with me, especially as I was about to embark on my very first location trip, to the Marina Mirage resort which had just opened in Port Douglas.

Trips are considered one of the biggest perks when you work at a fashion magazine, but in my experience they can also be one of the most difficult and fraught aspects of the job. Team dynamics are tricky, and when you throw in logistics, weather, budgets and personalities, the natural likelihood that things could go wrong generally means they will. But as trips go, this was one of the better ones: five sunny days at a five-star resort in Far North Queensland with two ridiculously good-looking male models who got so competitive during the shoot they would regularly stop what they were doing and challenge each other to see who could do the most push-ups.

Preparing the fashion for a shoot was so different in the late eighties and early nineties than it is today. The big luxury houses like Louis Vuitton, Gucci and Prada did not yet exist in Australia, and there were no press racks to borrow clothes from. Imported fashion had to be borrowed from department stores like the now-defunct Georges in Melbourne, or from smaller multi-brand boutiques like Trellini, Le Louvre and the Squire Shop in Sydney, which of course created a minefield of problems as it was actual stock, not samples. If you ruined something by, say, scorching it with an iron, smearing it with makeup, getting it wet or, even worse, if someone on the set went too close with a cigarette, it was a disaster.

In hindsight it was incredible training because you were taught to be fastidious with the clothes and accessories. I have no time for stylists who have no respect for the clothes they are handling, even if they're samples. Fashion editors working today now simply call in the clothes that they desire, usually from look books (photographs of all the pieces in a collection, shot on an in-house model) or their choice of a particular runway 'exit' (each individual look that was shown on the catwalk). In the case of local designers, they will go to showings to view a designer's collection and choose from what is there. But back then at *Vogue*, the fashion editors would have things specially made.

Australian designers represented the core of what was shot, because many of them were also our advertisers. Judith, and the other stylists at the time—Victoria 'Tory' Collison in Sydney and Mary Otte and Sandra Hirsh in the Melbourne office—would settle on a trend from the shows, and rather than just call the PRs and have it sent in (an option which simply didn't exist), they would make the rounds of their favourite Australian designers and explain the philosophy of the shoot and what they envisaged it would look like. This is not to say that designers were asked to copy things. It was a creative collaboration between the stylist and the designer. There would be long meetings complete with inspiration boards, art books, novels, fabrics and maps of exotic locations. Design houses such as Robert Burton, Trent Nathan, George Gross & Harry Who, Simona, Tea Rose, Jenny Bannister, Jenny Kee, Linda Jackson and Easton Pearson would create the most magical one-offs, and it was always a thrilling moment when they arrived at the office. No one really knew exactly what to expect, because designers could certainly go off brief. But when they got it right, you could see the vision being realised while the story came together before your eyes. And sometimes their 'off brief' took the shoot in a whole new and marvellous direction.

Bondi knitter John Macarthur could always be counted upon to conjure up the most wonderful handknitted sweaters and accessories. It was these types of spectacular pieces that were captioned 'Made to Order' for the reader who decided she couldn't live without a blue plastic mermaid dress. Young milliners such as the talented Annabel Ingall in Sydney and Tamasine Dale in Melbourne would create whimsical hats and headpieces, themed to suit. Judith always liked a hat. And a chunky knit. It was a way of approaching fashion shoots that was highly creative and original. It rarely happens today. No one has time to brief a designer, and the important international advertisers have to be accommodated first.

There was always a major issue with shoes: that being there weren't any. Judith's biggest lament was that there were not enough good shoes in Australia. We could borrow imports from the topnotch shoe emporium Evelyn Miles but, again, they were stock that had to be sold, so the soles were taped, taped and taped again to prevent wear and tear. The editors used to design the shoes or sandals they needed to complete their vision and then have them made by a small shoe factory in Melbourne. The *Vogue* fashion department's rabid attention to detail delivered me a sterling life lesson—if the shoe isn't right, then nothing is right.

Fashion assistants lived in fear of not having the correct shoe to present to the editor. Completed shoots were scrutinised by the senior editors through a magnifying loop in the art department, and the dreaded question would be asked through pursed lips: 'Was that the right shoe do you think?' If you heard that from June, Nancy or Judith, you were toast.

I walked into the fashion stockroom one day to find the new and gorgeous young fashion assistant Naomi Smith sitting on the floor, surrounded by literally hundreds of pairs of shoes. She turned to me, pale as a ghost, and said, 'The shoot is tomorrow. Apparently we don't have the right shoe'. I tried to joke her out of it, but tears were welling up in her eyes and I could sense the panic was rising. I comforted her by saying she had called in more shoes than I had ever seen. Judith would like one of them, surely?

'No, no, Kirstie, you don't understand. This is really, really serious. We don't have the right shoe,' she said gravely. 'We need a Louis heel.'

I pointed tentatively to a gold satin shoe I could see sticking out of the metre-high pile of options. 'Noooo!' she wailed. 'That's a kitten heel for god's sake!'

I felt so sorry for her and I walked back to my computer and typed out a piece of paper that said: 'No, this is really serious. We don't have the right shoe.' I then blew it up to poster size and taped it up on the wall in the fashion office. Fortunately Judith saw the humour in it, and decided one of Naomi's selections fit the bill, but shoes—to this day—remain a make or break factor in the world of high fashion. A well-chosen shoe adds proportion, modernity and newness to a look. Especially if you can't actually walk in it.

By 1988 my position at *Vogue* had changed. One day, while Nancy and I were shooting a promotion which required me to iron what seemed like four hundred white linen pants, shirts, jackets and skirts in an overheated studio, I had a mini meltdown. I loathe ironing. I'm terrible at it. I make more wrinkles than I take out. Back then, we used to iron everything to death. Now the art directors just take out every flaw in a photograph in post-production. I think I said something really pretentious to Nancy along the lines of, 'I'm too smart to iron for a living. My mother didn't raise me to do this.'

I probably would have shown me the door, but the gracious Nancy worked her magic back in the office, and convinced the powers that be to create a position for me that involved assisting the beauty editor Karin Upton, and writing fashion stories, headings and captions. It was my dream job—the majority of the role was writing, and I enjoyed the beauty world. It also meant the occasional shoot. It was everything I loved doing. I would have worked for free.

Naturally, like everything at *Vogue*, this move was not taken lightly. I was interviewed by June and asked to produce two designer profiles, a thousand words each, which would be duly appraised. I pounded them out with confidence and was offered the post.

The *Vogue* offices had relocated, leaving behind the character-filled office in Clarence Street and settling in a soulless new office building on the Pacific Highway in Greenwich, on Sydney's north shore. I was not a north shore girl, although a great deal of women who worked at *Vogue*, *Vogue Living* and the *Vogue Entertaining Guide* were. I detested that drive over the bridge. The move did compel me to buy my first car, a second-hand white Honda Civic that I later decorated with horribly kitsch, acrylic, zebra-fur seat covers. My initial application for a car loan was rejected because the bank manager didn't believe I earned enough to make the repayments. Being a young woman didn't help either.

My plight made it to the office of Aye Ling Koh, who was the magazine's chief financial officer, and who was both canny and down-to-earth. She asked me to drop by her office, so she could take a look at the sums. 'What assets did you tell them you have?' she asked. 'None. I don't have any,' I replied innocently. 'Oh no, c'mon girl!' she exclaimed. Aye Ling drove a Porsche and was reportedly on her way to owning most of Chatswood. Aye Ling used to goodheartedly lecture the fashion girls about not spending all our salaries on clothes and how we should think about real estate. It went in one ear and out the other for most of us, as we rationalised spending two thousand dollars on some new must-have, but bless her for trying.

Twenty years later I would find myself doing a similar thing, nagging my fashion editors to 'Admire the Proenza Schouler jacket, yes, by all means, but why don't you top up your superannuation instead?' It still falls on deaf ears.

I was now installed in the fashion office, privy to all the conversations, the fun, the hysteria and the drama. We were not highly staffed by any means, so it was vital to work together and keep the bitching to a minimum in order to get through the workload. At any given period there would be a fashion director, one or two fashion editors, one fashion assistant and an office coordinator. Normally there would be only one editor in beauty, but because Karin and I could write across all areas the department was expanded.

Karin proved to be a wonderful mentor and colleague. She was elegant and attractive, expensively dressed and wildly materialistic on the outside, but underneath she was witty and generous and quite self-deprecating. She owned the job of beauty editor, investing it with unparalleled glamour and importance.

Karin was renowned for driving a black vintage Mercedes with quilted seats while wearing white leather driving gloves. Her hair and nails were always perfect. Her wardrobe consisted of Yves Saint Laurent, Chanel and Armani. She smoked St Moritz menthols in her office and constantly drank Diet Coke out of a wine glass, leaving a perpetual red lipstick mark. She was larger than life.

Beauty advertising far outstripped fashion advertising at that time, and our area was crucial. I began to attend beauty functions either with Karin or on her behalf, mingling with other magazine editors and our advertisers. I started to understand exactly how the relationship between client and journalist worked, and how to work a creative vision into that equation for the reader. You cannot make an impactful or interesting product if you are merely regurgitating a press release, or being coerced into covering something you consider inappropriate. An editor or journalist has to go the extra distance and work out a new angle, a new spin, and in some cases push back and say no, let's think of something else. It is what the reader deserves. It's not a popular viewpoint today, but I do believe there is a middle ground that can be found where everyone wins.

Vogue's publisher was Lesley Wild, who was tough, brash and confident. She certainly had her battles with the editorial team in the cut and thrust that comes with that role but she was damn good at her job, the clients loved her, and she had respect for the magazine's editorial integrity. There seems to be a common perception today that editors who have regard for the consumer are arrogant dinosaurs, standing in the way of 'commerciality'. But I question what will be considered 'commercial' about zero sales when the intelligent and sceptical reader realises full well you sold out, in order to please an advertiser.

The chairman of Condé Nast in Australia was Bernard Leser, who had originally founded *Vogue Australia* in 1959. He was based in the Condé Nast offices in New York, but would regularly visit Sydney and was often seen leaping out of his car (with driver) sporting a safari suit. He had a particularly fetching one in pale blue that Judith loved, given her penchant for creating shoots around them. Bernie, as he was known, was a true gentleman, with his shock of white hair and mellifluous voice. He had old-school charm. But by 1989 it seemed that there was now a perceptible shift in the priorities of management.

June's *Vogue* had always been very arts focused, with a major amount of excellent editorial devoted to theatre, books, film, dance and opera. I was not privy to the exact reasons for the change of guard, but I suspect the all-encompassing and conveniently amorphous 'commerciality' argument played a part. It always does. Unless you are an axe-wielding psycho and need to be escorted off the premises, most exits come down to money. In fact, if profits were significantly up, I suggest even a psycho and their axe could stay and be given a bonus.

Suddenly, June and Eve were ousted and a new managing director installed, Verne Westerburg, who hailed from US Condé Nast. Nancy Pilcher was given the position of editor, and a new era began.

I had taken over most of the fashion writing at that point, which was reasonably daunting given I was following in the very impressive footsteps of Marion von Adlerstein, who had moved to predominately writing travel. Marion had been an advertising copywriter before she joined *Vogue* and she was crack-hot at the perfect par. I always remember one heading, or what is called a 'pull out', on a Spanish flamenco-inspired fashion story where she wrote: 'The lines of a dress, as emphatic as the click of stiletto heels on a tiled floor.' And for a menswear story: 'In this suit, you'll get the job, the girl and the table.' I think witty copy on a fashion page is a must. I've always laboured over them. Cover lines such as 'Great shoes and bags!' are a terrible, tired cop out.

Adding to the pressure of being even half as good as Marion was the fact we had to write to character count. It seems unbelievable now, but in those days there were still no computers in the art department. Layouts were done on paper, and copy was pasted on using bromides—type that had been painstakingly cut out with a scalpel and stuck down. There was some sort of medieval-style box contraption and the artists would thrust their hands in to spray the glue on the pages. In retrospect it was an occupational health and safety nightmare but, then again, so were all the staff who chain-smoked cigarettes in the office until the laws banned it.

In order that the art layout not be changed too frequently, writers had to be character perfect. Unfortunately, *Vogue Italia* layouts had become a design benchmark, and were frequently referenced, so I would end up having to form a heading that had words of one letter, two, two and then three. I did try to explain to the art department that the English language was a little more limited than Italian in terms of words of one or two letters. But I also tried my hardest to fit the layouts, and I was very proud when one day the impeccably mannered art assistant Eric Matthews came to my desk and awarded me The Golden Scalpel Award for Exactitude. Fortunately the very talented art director Christina Zimpel went on a calligraphy binge for headings, using decorative script hand drawn by her artist husband Patric Shaw, so he would work with what I wrote instead of the other way round.

With such a varied, smart and opinionated group of people working in one office on tight deadlines, it was natural that things could sometimes be fraught, but the camaraderie between the team was strong and supportive. The media portrayal of women who work at fashion magazines has always painted us being bitchy and catty towards each other. It exists, definitely, but do bitchy, catty environments not exist in other businesses? Given the amount of unsubstantiated, puerile mud-slinging I've witnessed emanating from other media outlets over the years, fashion magazine environments seem like a somewhat Sapphic utopia in comparison. At the core of these stereotypes is a tired belief that all women in fashion are shallow, lazy, pea-brained and self-serving. And yes, there are some. But from what I have observed they never last the distance. It's a very, very tough business.

Putting the magazine out each month, to the exacting standard that was expected, was damn hard work. The office juniors would almost always work back until 9 or 10 p.m. On many occasions I would put my head in the stockroom to check on Naomi, worried that she was going to be smothered, *Extreme Hoarders*-style, by the raft of suitcases that would arrive from the Melbourne office each day, filled with John Smedley sweaters, Comme des Garcons skirts and kilos of jewellery from Castalia Antiques. As the fashion assistant in the early nineties, Naomi had to suffer through the fashion period where everything was piled high with multiple necklaces, bracelets, rings and earrings. Judith was in a 'navy Armani jacket and a batik skirt, put back with silver ethnic necklaces and oversized amber beads' moment, and the jewellery influx was torturous. One earring lost in a sea of tissue paper could cost you your job. Luckily, fashions winds shifted not long afterwards and years of minimalism followed, where one lone Elsa Peretti bangle from Tiffany was often sufficient.

Given that our bosses were some of the chicest women in the country, the junior staff also, by osmosis, began to imitate the way they dressed. We'd arrived on the first day in what we thought were our best clothes, only to be swiftly influenced by their sartorial style, albeit on our tiny budgets. If you wanted to be rich, it was best not to work at *Vogue*. Nancy, who owned a vast wardrobe of designer clothes, very generously gave me a navy Giorgio Armani jacket, knowing I couldn't afford one. I wore that jacket for years until I finally had to retire it because it had gone shiny from too much dry-cleaning, but it made me feel so *Vogue*. I remember looking around the fashion office once and we were all wearing navy jackets, with white Hanes or Fruit of the Loom t-shirts from the US, batik-sarong skirts, amber beads and woven tote bags from Bali, with silver-hoop earrings. Still not a bad look today, in fact.

There was a white shirt or t-shirt under a little strappy black dress phase too, which was rather random in hindsight, but we all played along with that. There was the full-length, silk taffeta skirt, put back with a crisp white shirt and a wide belt for evening: that was easy and economical because you could have a dressmaker whip you up one.

There was also a platform gym boot trend embraced only by fashion editor Tory Collison.

I loved Tory; she was utterly consumed with fashion. Never a victim—she is far, far more stylish than that—but if she loved something, she had to have it. We worked together for years. I once called her from the Gucci store in Milan to ask her if she wanted me to buy her the latest must-have Gucci shoe. It was the floral, round-toed, sling-back sandal from Tom Ford's Cher-inspired collection. She was pregnant with her first child and couldn't make it to the shows. 'Yes, yes,' she said excitedly after I told her how much they would cost.

'What size are you again, Tors?' I asked.

She replied,'36 and a half. But if they don't have that, anything from a 35 to a 37 will do'. Tory was so crazy about fashion she often bought things that didn't fit.

I did buy the shoes for her and a few weeks later, popped them on her feet while she was in bed in the maternity ward. She probably never wore them anyway because, truth be told, I bought a pair too and they hurt like hell.

2

LOCATION, LOCATION

Until the launch of other competitive titles such as *Marie Claire, Elle* and *Harper's Bazaar* in Australia, *Vogue* had few rivals at the luxury end of the market. Since its inception, every page in *Vogue* had been created from scratch, not lifted from other Condé Nast titles overseas, so costs were always closely watched. We certainly never operated with anywhere near the budgets of our sister publications internationally. The team always strived to be just as excellent though, and this often came down to plain old Aussie resourcefulness.

Vogue Australia has always championed the Australian model, and there were many beautiful local girls who became an extended part of the *Vogue* family: beauties such as Sarah O'Hare (now Murdoch), Gillian (née Mather) Bailey, Anneliese Seubert, Jenny Hayman, Kate Fischer, Ruve, Kristy Hinze and Emma Balfour. Photographers such as Monty Coles, Grant Matthews, Richard Bailey and Graham Shearer were also in the club, as were all their preferred hair and makeup artists. At times the dynamics had the same amount of family dysfunction, angst and emotion as a Christmas Day lunch.

Karin and I set up our own large-scale beauty shoots almost every month using local talent, which is a luxury in publishing today. Our impetus was to promote a new beauty product or trend, but the larger goal was to establish a certain style of Australian beauty, rather than just mimic how Linda Evangelista looked in the latest *Vogue Italia*.

Editorial budgets have been reduced so drastically that shooting beauty in this way went by the wayside years ago. The expectation now is that an editor will pick up beauty shots from international syndication instead. While it's true that this reduces costs, it also means the magazine is no longer a platform to showcase the creativity of Australia's best hair and makeup artists, and it limits the work for Australia's top beauty models and photographers. Karin produced a seminal beauty shoot for *Vogue Australia*'s thirtieth anniversary issue in 1989, featuring Elle Macpherson and shot by photographer Graham Shearer on location in Broome. Elle later recounted that the resultant work 'was just unbelievable. Graham was at his peak … and we did pictures I hadn't done before. I think *Vogue* were the first people that used me for beauty and not just for body'. Naomi Smith was the assistant on the trip, and recalls that when the 4WD became bogged on the bank of a tidal river, Elle nonchalantly dived into crocodile-infested waters and swam for help.

Australian models have always been good sports. They are such brilliant team players, never taking themselves too seriously. And they always loved doing Aussie *Vogue*, knowing how proud their families would be.

One memorable beauty shoot with Graham at Bondi Icebergs pool came with its own set of problems when we were shooting New Zealand supermodel Rachel Hunter. Graham had decided, for reasons unknown, that a wall of gigantic ice bricks should be built behind her as she posed next to the pool. Given that it was February, the ice was melting as soon as it was stacked, so more and more ice needed to be delivered by truck. At one point I was sitting in the location van with the very young and spectacular Rachel, waiting for construction to finish, and she said to me, apropos of nothing, 'I'm going to marry a rock star'. Obviously the likelihood of her luring one was rather high, and she did in fact go on to marry the middle-aged Rod Stewart, who I guess counts as a rock star. I have no idea how we made the tenuous connection to a melting ice wall in the beauty pages. Probably 'Winter Glamour' or something suitably oblique. Locations for shoots were normally decided between the photographer and the stylist, and could be either literal, as in say, silks and brocades ('I see Turkey!'), or contradictory, as in ballgowns in a car park.

For another story, Karin and I travelled to the Hyatt Regency Coolum in Queensland to shoot a spa-inspired story with model Emma Balfour. We would aim to produce ten or twelve conceptual beauty photographs, covering topics such as massage, hands, feet, hair, hydration, yoga and so on, that could then be used over a long period of time to illustrate stories as they came up. The photographer was a prickly American who had a tendency to turn nasty towards other, usually more junior, members of the team. The resort had just been completed and the foliage was in early stages, so the property was bakingly hot, and the only way to get around was by painfully-slow electric buggy. All the clothes and props were in my room and we had decided to shoot near the beach, which was pretty much the furthermost point you could go on the buggy.

At one stage during the shoot, the photographer decided he needed something that was back in the room. I was dispatched, and returned some twenty minutes later. He then requested something else. Again, I dutifully ran the errand. The heat was unbearable and the sun at the perfect point in the sky to be blinding. Then something else was requested. I knew what he was doing. Over the years I have witnessed various degrees of bullying by photographers, because on a shoot, they are considered God. Not because they possess any God-like qualities in particular, that's for sure, but because you need them to succeed and take the best shots possible. You have to come back with the goods. I appreciate the pressure on them is intense, but the humiliation of other members of the team is never necessary.

After the fifth or sixth time he ordered me back for some dubious reason, and even though I felt dreadful for leaving Karin there, I parked the buggy, locked the door of my room and didn't return. I've never had the patience or the personality to put up with tantrums, or to be manipulated. Fashion editors, it seems, have an ability to endure psychological torture as part of their job; I have huge admiration for them. I saw some awful behaviour from a lot of photographers and a few models when I was in the position of assistant, and it put me off ever becoming a fashion stylist myself. That, and the fact that I'm crap at it.

I soon found myself in the very fortunate position of being able to go on most of the location trips, both fashion and beauty, because I stretched across all areas—I could assist the fashion editor, style a beauty shoot (because few clothes are required) and write the attendant travel story. It was economical to send me.

One of my first fashion trips was, once again to Queensland, this time in the tropical hinterlands of Surfers Paradise, with photographer Grant Matthews and fashion editor Tory Collison. Despite her petite size, exquisite manners and blonde good looks, Tory is one of the most tenacious, dogged and determined fashion editors one could ever encounter. She is never satisfied, and her relentless quest for perfection in a photograph, or indeed in everything, is equal parts inspiring and exhausting. The outcome is always worth it. But if anything can go wrong for Tory, it will. A desert salt plain that has seen no rain for years will flood the day she arrives to set up. If a hostile alien spaceship were to visit Earth, it would land on Tory's shoot location. I used to call it the 'Tory principle', which is 'if it's not one thing, it's another'. But despite the incessant calamities, Tory always keeps her sense of humour, and forges ahead undeterred.

On one particular day of this shoot we had the model standing in the water at the top of a rocky waterfall, which would have been at least ten to fifteen metres high. Tory waded in to adjust something on the girl's outfit, with her model pack filled with pins and clamps strapped around her waist, when suddenly she slipped, went under, was swept up by the current and disappeared over the edge of the cliff. The whole crew looked at each other in horror, mouths agape. Grant quickly threw his camera aside and thrashed his way through the scrub to look over the edge while we all stood in grim silence, expecting the worst. I was sure she was dead, dashed on the rocks—a fashion casualty.

Then came the sounds of Tory in fits of laughter. There she was at the bottom of the waterfall, sodden but unhurt. We all burst into relieved hysterics and cheered her on as she clambered her way back up to the top, doing a hand-over-foot commando climb Bear Grylls would have been impressed with.

'You have to be more careful, Tors!' admonished Grant. He was always the grown-up on a shoot. The hilarity subsided, we thanked our lucky stars and continued on with taking the shot. Tors, once again, ventured in to tweak the clothes. And we all watched in disbelief as—in what felt like slow motion—she slipped and shot over the edge once again. This time we all laughed like drains.

I have another indelible memory of that trip, shooting in the late afternoon sun on the main beach of Surfers Paradise. The model was leggy Australian beauty Jenny Hayman, all long, tanned limbs, swan neck, big smile and short cropped blonde hair. Jenny was cute and uncomplicated, and one of *Vogue*'s most popular models.

As she was cavorting around on the sand, happily dancing in a long skirt, a young couple who were taking a walk along the beach approached. The boy, who would have been in his late teens or early twenties, glanced shyly at Jenny, naturally enough. His girlfriend, who was dumpy and plain, shot a death stare at him. 'Wayne,' she growled. 'Wayne, stop lookin' at her. Don't look. She just loves herself.' She delivered this with her eyes downcast, focused firmly on the sand. I found it funny, and very Aussie, but at the same time, poignant. It is a not uncommon attitude towards high fashion and beauty, one that speaks volumes about a person's self-esteem. We all admired Jenny as a vision of loveliness and that's what the photographs were celebrating. But beauty can challenge some people. Poor Wayne. His girlfriend felt threatened and therefore wouldn't allow him to rest his eyes on something extraordinary for a few seconds.

It was the early nineties and tragically the fashion industry had been struck hard with too many deaths due to HIV/AIDS. Many of *Vogue*'s preferred hair and makeup artists passed away: huge talents like Robbie Snow, Nick Zeigler and Stephen Price. Another great, Aaron, drank himself to death after the passing of his beloved mother. Stephen Price was the hairdresser on the Queensland shoot, and he bravely revealed to the team one night at dinner that he had just been diagnosed with HIV. It was mostly a death sentence back then. No one said a word. Grant simply reached for his hand and we all joined hands around the table while Stephen cried, but not for long. He looked up, sniffed, got the usual cheeky look back on his face, made some rude joke, and we didn't discuss it again, bless him.

I adored accompanying Tory on trips, even though I admit I was probably close to the world's worst assistant. It was becoming reasonably apparent that I prefer to tell people what to do, rather than be told. But dear Tors seemed to overlook that. She even took over the ironing, which she actually likes and excels at. She irons tea towels at home.

One of our best trips together was a voyage on the brand-new *Club Med 2* cruise ship, which sailed from New Caledonia to Vanuatu and the Isle of Pines. Sarah O'Hare was the model, a 21-year-old ex-ballet dancer who had begun her modelling career at *Vogue* in her teens. Sarah had the most perfect, flawless skin, thick blonde curls and an athletic, yet curvy, body—a complete knockout. She also has a kooky sense of humour, which is always a bonus on long trips.

When we boarded I made a point of telling Sarah not to use her mobile phone, as the satellite dish on the ship meant calls would be incredibly costly, and *Vogue* would not pay the bill. But she confessed to me she was missing her boyfriend at the time, and I noticed that when we were not shooting she would often be on her phone.

The light was so strong that Graham could only shoot first thing in the morning and again at sunset, which left us all a lot of free time in between. Graham was a keen windsurfer, so quite a few hours were filled in either surfing or waterskiing. I never gave it a moment's thought that we were in the middle of the Pacific Ocean, until the Tahitian waterski instructor took me to the stern of the boat after dinner one night and pointed over the railing to the ocean below. The kitchen was throwing out fish scraps. Eerily illuminated by the strong spotlight were four huge sharks feeding furiously. I shuddered. The instructors had been dragging dozens of happily unsuspecting Japanese waterskiers through shark-infested waters all week, none of whom I ever saw even stand up.

Fashion trips were always quite intrepid. We got so caught up in our fashion bubble that we were often stupidly oblivious to our surrounds and their hidden dangers. In the Isle of Pines we went very far inland into dense forest to shoot inside a dank, watery cave. At one point, a native Kanak arrived and stood watching us closely for almost an hour, stony-faced and almost naked, holding a huge curved machete. And we just kept shooting. Nowadays there are so many occupational health and safety regulations that they want you to predict how many power cords might potentially be tripped over. It's so bureaucratic it's better to 'don't ask, don't tell' or just drop the idea entirely. Can you imagine an occupational health and safety officer's face when you confess that your fashion director was nearly eaten by a lion in Botswana because her hair got caught in the Velcro opening of the tent?

Fortunately, we made it back to the boat, and the shoot—with Sarah looking impeccable in fifties-style fashion, with slicked-back hair and bright-red lipstick—was one of her best ever for *Vogue*. Just before the ship docked, the staff presented me with her phone bill. I handed it to Sarah as the team all met for sunset drinks to toast the success of the shoot. It was close to $8000. Sarah, to her credit, lay back on a lounge chair deathly pale for a couple of moments, took a few deep breaths, and said: 'Oh well.' We not only all made it back alive but Nancy loved the shoot, and Sarah made the cover of the June 1993 edition.

In addition to the various disasters that could and would happen on a major trip, there was always the very great possibility that the editor-in-chief would not like the results. There was huge pressure to deliver something phenomenal, because location trips obviously ate up most of the magazine's monthly editorial budget. Melbourne fashion editor Mary Otte once did an entire issue with one male and two female models, shot all around Australia, from Tasmania to Broome and Far North Queensland. It was a mammoth effort and the photographs, taken by Graham Shearer again, were well received by all the team in the fashion office, but the then editor June McCallum didn't like them for some mysterious styling reasons.

Fashion editors feel devastated when their shoots are rejected because they have obsessed over every tiny detail to get to the end result. It is almost impossible for them to be objective. Mary composed a very calm email to June stating that if she had to do it over again she would make the exact same decisions, and then promptly resigned, which I always thought was tremendously chic.

During Judith Cook's time as fashion director she once chose Africa as the prime destination for a major issue. There was so much excitement in the stockroom as all the fabulous pieces she had collaborated on began to flow in. There were black-and-white zebra toe thongs with black fringing, ocelot-print parasols with cane handles, voluminous handpainted Maasai-inspired ballgowns in brilliant red, gorgeous safari suits in black linen, and piles of colourful beads and bracelets and cuffs. Naomi was the assistant, and as with any trip to Africa it was arduous, expensive and thrilling.

After the team were safely home, the photographs duly arrived in to the art department and the verdict began to trickle through the building. Nancy hated them. She thought the model was spectacularly unattractive.

It's unusual that such a major trip went ahead without the model being approved, but often when an international model is booked direct to a location, how they look when they turn up is not quite how they were depicted in their portfolio. They can often carry a few extra kilos in weight that the agent chose not to divulge, and the fashion editor then faces the dilemma of having none of the clothes fit. On many occasions, Judith had to cut clothes up the back and pin them together.

In the case of the African incident, Judith was disconsolate. 'I liked her. I specifically chose her because she looked like a lioness!' she exclaimed. I think I gently suggested to her that perhaps therein lay the problem. The story was cut drastically and there was a mad scramble for African artifacts and a Maasai backdrop, while a studio shoot was then set up in downtown Sydney Central with a different model. The Africa issue managed to make it to print, but we were reminded about the cost by our editorial business manager for years afterwards, even if we hadn't personally been involved.

The sheer unpredictability of location trips and the personalities of the chosen crew certainly provided a myriad of dramas. In Greece, fashion editor Sandra Hirsh learned the hard way when her model, a rising star who had won an international modelling competition from Germany, took a shine to the photographer's assistant. It happened a lot.

Photographers' assistants are, generally speaking, always really hot, and they are more appealing than the photographer because they don't get cross with you. Strangely, the photographer's assistant is often better looking than the male model. They're not so model-y. Apparently, after an early team dinner, while Sandra thought everyone was safely tucked up in bed, the model and the assistant went for a post-Retsina spin on a motorcycle and had an accident on gravel. The poor girl's face was split open, and in the midst of her agent threatening to sue, the runner-up in the modelling contest was quickly dispatched.

There were different problems on the idyllic Fijian island of Vatulele, where I joined Judith as assistant and travel writer. The photographer was Richard Bailey, a handsome, charming young surfer from the northern beaches who would continue to work exclusively for *Vogue Australia* for more than two decades, until his passing from cancer in 2010. Everything was postcard perfect—pale blue water, a palm-fringed beach with pristine white sands, glorious weather, the whole cliché. The model arrived from the US, a gamine beauty who resembled a young Audrey Hepburn. We had trunkloads of clothes; we were poised for a classic *Vogue* shoot. What could go wrong?

After an afternoon reconnaissance we all met for dinner, and noticed the model seemed unusually quiet. Almost melancholy. We put it down to the long flights and regrouped the next morning. Richard started to shoot and she became more and more sad. She wouldn't smile and was on the brink of tears the whole time. At one point, standing knee-deep in the azure ocean, dressed in a sarong and gigantic straw hat and looking like a divine aquatic goddess, she burst into sobs. Richard was so frustrated. We called her agency in New York to ask what the hell was going on. There's nothing quite like being told by a supercilious model booker, when you are on a remote island in the Pacific and expected to produce an entire summer issue, that the model they sent you 'has had a very troubled upbringing. She's got a lot of issues. And she hates modelling.'

None of us were without sympathy but we all had a job to do, and you never know whether the story you are getting is straight. For all we knew, the real story was that she missed her boyfriend. I worked with a model once who cried for the entire day because her cat had died. We had to keep redoing her makeup. I must admit I'm not a cat person, but by all accounts it had expired two days before. How long is one expected to put up with cat grief?

Given that a large amount of pages were expected from the Vatulele trip, Judith creatively improvised and came up with a tenuous narrative about the model meeting someone called Captain Jack (which just so happened to be Richard's handsome and amiable assistant Mike, again proving the theory that they are far more useful than male models), so we shot him as much as humanly possible to pad the story out. The narrative of a shoot is always discussed and decided beforehand, but a professional team has to roll with the punches. Our shoot had moved from ethereal tropic nymph emerges from the crystalline water to *South Pacific: The Musical*. Just our luck, heavy tropical rain arrived and the skies were leaden for days, so we all began having tequila slammers at 3 p.m. just to get through. Despite the series of challenges, the photographs turned out beautifully.

While we loved to promote Australian models, we also needed variety. We were shooting at least four main-page stories per issue, and readers tired quickly of seeing the same models too frequently. Given that *Vogue Australia* was a long way off the global fashion radar back then, we could not simply pick up the phone and book the top models in the world, like Linda Evangelista, Christy Turlington and Cindy Crawford. If we were able to secure girls of that level it was through long and complex negotiations, usually with a third party that had a vested interest, like a fashion or beauty advertiser. Given these parameters, we were often using girls who were very young and just starting out, or in some cases, a few who were a little bit past their prime. That meant in their late twenties. The ageism is not quite so strict now.

Tory and I once made a reasonably disastrous trip to Los Angeles to produce two shoots: the first with a very top model, who, truth be told, had probably slipped a peg or two down the ladder of fame. When she arrived at the sumptuous Beverly Hills Peninsula Hotel where we were staying, she clearly felt there were better things she could be doing. By the end of the day, I would have suggested retirement.

Three hours late for a call time of 8 a.m., she sauntered into the suite where we had all the fashion and accessories laid out for her to try on, got into the bed, picked up the phone and dialled room service nachos. Tory and I nearly fainted. We were never, ever allowed to order room service on trips; it was a no-no, except in extreme circumstances, say, if you had lost the use of your legs. We had very rigid rules: no mini bar, no personal laundry, no personal telephone calls, no alcohol. The budgets for food were frugal to say the least. It was common at dinners for the photographers' assistants to order three courses, given they were usually strapping young men and they'd been working hard all day. When this happened, it generally followed that Tory and I would stare at each other with barely suppressed panic and then say airily, 'Oh, I think I'll just have a salad', so we could keep the bill down. It wasn't worth the torture we would endure from

Patricia Watson, the business manager, when we got back. Tory could survive for days on Diet Coke.

Back to our pensioner/model, who then decided to chain-smoke cigarettes and refused to put them out while we tried on clothes. In between shots she would return to the bed and spill corn chips all over the 1000 thread-count Egyptian cotton sheets. She was as animated and engaged as a basket of laundry. Eventually we brought in a male model who was so insanely buff that she brightened up enough to take a decent picture, but all we wanted to do was to pour the (uneaten as it turned out) nachos over Nana's head, as I had taken to calling her.

For the next shoot we had booked a sixteen-year-old girl who was purportedly the agency's next big thing. We had seen her model card and some amateur test shots, and she certainly had something: pouty, blonde and innocent. She and her mother met us at the hotel and we were dismayed to see the first problem. She had thick ankles. Either we had not seen a head-to-toe shot, or it had been doctored. Fashion editors are fanatical about girls having good legs. Even Cyd Charisse probably would have struggled to get through at a *Vogue* casting.

But what was truly distressing was that it became obvious the women were in dire financial straits. Her mother had driven from we weren't sure where, and we noticed that her beaten-up sedan was full of personal possessions. They were living in the car. The girl ordered chilli for lunch and was surprised at how it tasted, because she told us she had only ever had it from a can. We didn't have the budget to put them up for more than one night, but it was clear the mother saw her daughter's burgeoning career as their ticket out of poverty. Sadly, that was unlikely to happen because her calves weren't ever going to be slim enough.

Apart from the various fashion trips I had managed to insinuate myself into, there were also opportunities for travel that related to beauty shoots and stories. Fortunately for me, Karin did not like to travel excessively, while I on the other hand was willing to hang onto the wing of a plane, especially if it meant going to the US.

In 1992, a press trip or 'junket' to San Francisco had been offered to *Vogue*, and Nancy decided that I could take the trip, and then fly on to New York to do two beauty shoots, which would hopefully also produce two covers. I was nervous, but ecstatic. Thirty years old and my first trip to America. Business-class. I remember literally skipping across Rushcutters Bay Park that night I was so happy. I'd never been on a press junket before, and I quickly learnt an irrefutable fact—there will always be one major dickhead in the party who will ruin the entire experience for you.

On this particular occasion it was a newspaper journalist, who wasn't even a travel writer. I suspect his editor had given him the trip to get him out of the office and give the rest of the staff a break from his inane rambling. He commenced proceedings by getting totally pissed in the departure lounge, topping himself up to almost-legless status once we were in the air. He was so smashed by the time we lined up at customs and immigration in the US, he started swaying, swearing and complaining about American imperialism at the top of his voice. Always a sensible call in the States.

The debonair PR representative who was accompanying our group was mortified and, I sensed, ready to put him on the first plane back, but unfortunately he remained with us for the four days we spent in San Francisco. His crowning achievement came on the last night when we were dining at one of the city's finest establishments, and the very famous chef came out specially to run through the menu with us, dish by dish. As he finished the intricate explanations, the moron took a breath and said, 'Yeah, but do you have any spag bol?' waiting for the huge laughs that surprisingly did not spill from our clenched jaws. From then on I vowed I would avoid junkets at all costs, but at times I have been obliged to join them. And there would usually be someone I wanted to strangle.

From San Francisco I continued on to New York, and arrived at La Guardia late at night, laden with suitcases. The very chi chi Mark Hotel had just opened uptown, and I checked into the vast presidential suite on the top floor, which had glittering views all the way downtown. There was jazz playing on the brand-new CD player. I was in heaven. For the umpteenth time in my career at *Vogue*, I took a minute to appreciate how privileged I was.

The phone rang. It was the general manager of the hotel. Would I care to have dinner the following night? The writer Paul Theroux would be joining us. I nearly wept when I had to decline because I was expected at a perfume launch. It is something we were all taught as juniors. You never blew something off because you got a better offer. *Vogue* staff have always been expected to attend everything they are invited to, no excuses. That is your job, first and foremost. I have seen other journalists throughout the years be incredibly cavalier with their invitations and appointments and it has always infuriated me. The invitations come because of the job, not because you're so special.

The two beauty stories I shot that week in New York ultimately did produce covers and both taught me a great deal. One, with model Daniela Pestova, was a triumph. The shot was upbeat and she was reader-friendly, in that she was able to appear glamorous yet approachable. I had even managed to magically choose the right earrings to match the Simona silk blouse. (Styling on my own was always hit and miss.) It was one of our biggest-selling covers ever.

The other cover was taken from an arty black-and-white hair story I did with a humourless Swedish photographer, who was very talented but the last word in arrogant. He studiously ignored me all day on the shoot, conferring only with the surly British makeup artist who kept calling me Kylie on purpose, despite me correcting her umpteen times. The pictures were gorgeous, the model resonating with a vintage glamour not unlike that of Marlene Dietrich. A shot of her wearing long, black, satin gloves was chosen for the next cover. I was on a roll. What a triumph! Kirstie took on New York and won! Was Australia big enough for me now?

But the black-and-white glamour cover was a complete flop with readers. Sales were dismal. And thus I learned the lesson that is an editor's greatest truism: you are only ever as good as your last cover.

3

THE BUSINESS OF BEAUTY

By the early nineties I had become the beauty editor, a position that afforded me many glamorous experiences. 'Beauty' is great training ground for an editor-in-chief, because it's intrinsically commercial. I don't think I'm revealing state secrets when I say we were there to help an advertiser sell their moisturiser. Fashion is much more subjective, and emotional, whereas the health and beauty area is more logical. Bearing in mind that my job was to rationalise spending $1500 on a face cream. That's logic, *Vogue*-style.

I was expected to give our advertisers coverage in the magazine, of course, but I also had free reign to promote anything I desired. Our Melbourne fashion editor Sandra Hirsh telephoned me one day and mentioned that she knew a young girl, Poppy King, who had a small lipstick line I might like to take a look at. Poppy came in to see me, a tiny eighteen-year-old blonde with alabaster skin and the darkest matte red lips I'd ever seen outside Kabuki theatre. She had come up with the idea of seven super-matte dark red and brown lipsticks that contained double the pigment you could find in other lipsticks. You couldn't find the shades at other companies, certainly not with the dramatic impact of her lip colours. Poppy showed me a few worse-for-wear samples, which she pulled out of a small makeup bag. I thought the idea was genius, and that she was certainly her own best publicity angle. I called to set up an appointment with the beauty buyer at David Jones and of course wrote a piece in *Vogue*. The rest is history, as the Poppy lipstick brand became an enormous success both here and in the US. That's the sort of impact that editorial with a real and honest angle can make.

The late eighties and early nineties were heady times for international beauty companies, who were spending up big on launches and press trips. At one very extravagant lunch at the Museum of Contemporary Art in Sydney, for the launch of an at-home hair colour, I was seated next to the taciturn managing director who was clearly bored out of his brain and mentally calculating how much this was costing him, as the beauty editors were showered with champagne, gifts and themed desserts. After numerous speeches, videos and live models displaying their shiny beautiful locks he turned to me and said, 'Don't you think all of this is just stupid?' I was taken aback for a moment, because I thought, 'Yes, it is a gigantic waste of time', but I was enjoying myself immensely. What I actually said however was: 'Well, the amount of money, planning and effort that has gone into this event clearly demonstrates how important this product launch is on your marketing calendar, and is a good indication as to how much editorial you will be expecting us to produce for you.' Which is the truth. The beauty editor just happens to be in the very fortunate position of having all this largesse reign down on her personally, while the implicit business agreement takes place.

It was his turn to look taken aback, but he agreed with me. He resigned not long after. Chatting to twenty-something beauty editors while they scoff down cream cakes at lavish lunches clearly wasn't his thing.

I loved writing beauty copy, because a degree of wit and ingenuity is required to make an eye shadow palette sound exciting to the reader. It became slightly more challenging when advertisers had an expectation of a two-thousand-word article on a night serum. This is another tacit commercial exchange: you interview someone from their 'laboratory' and then produce an article insinuating that the cream may miraculously change the molecular structure of skin and resist gravity. The hugely powerful Estée Lauder Group was *Vogue*'s biggest advertiser, and early on in my beauty editorship I was 'Laudered'. They created the benchmark on how to do things with style, and happily that company does have a state-of-the-art research facility, so there was real science to draw on.

In 1992 I was flown to New York, collected by limousine at the airport and whisked into a top hotel uptown, near the Lauder offices on Fifth Avenue. I checked into my suite to discover bags and bags of expensive lotions and potions, perfume and makeup waiting for me. There were tickets to The Frick Collection and The Whitney Museum on the desk, and a huge wooden box filled with exotic fruits from 'The Fruit of the Month Club'. I was informed by handwritten note on a thick, creamy card that dinner was booked at the renowned restaurant Daniel that evening, where I would be joined by a Lauder representative.

The following day I visited the plush Lauder corporate offices, housed in the General Motors building on Fifth Avenue. I met and chatted with the lovely Evelyn Lauder, the wife of Estée's son Leonard, in the 'Lauder' rooms which were floral and feminine, with blue sofas and drapes, fine china teacups, pretty flowers and silver bowls. I was then taken to the Clinique offices where everything was white and minimal, and I was given a notepad with pale-green pencils and a glass of chilled water. Afterwards we moved on to Prescriptives, which was the new whizz-bang brand in their stable, its personality reflected in the matte-grey surrounds and the modernist coffee mugs. The New West rooms (an Estée Lauder line that has since folded) were all Sante Fe, with cactuses and bright colours. I was waiting for them to break out the tequila.

The attention to detail, the manners, and the professionalism was mind-blowing. I knew I was at the centre of one of the truly great American companies. I was 'Laudered' many times over the years, but I have never forgotten that first one. After my office visit, I was taken to lunch at uptown Cipriani's by Rebecca McGreevy, Lauder's senior vice president of PR, an impeccable Southern woman in her sixties who was charm personified. At one point during the meal she said calmly, 'I have a rather big surprise for you. Estée Lauder is going to join you and me for afternoon tea later today at The Plaza.'

My jaw dropped. Estée Lauder was elderly and reportedly in poor health. She had not made a public appearance for quite some time. To be given the opportunity to meet the legendary Estée herself was extraordinary. I rushed back to my room after lunch and hurriedly prepared a list of questions, and changed my clothes three times. I was going to meet Estée Lauder for heaven's sake, the founder of the company, an icon: everything had to be perfect.

I arrived on the appointed hour at The Plaza, and could see Mrs Lauder and Rebecca seated at a table behind the palm fronds on the ground floor. An orchestra was playing 'The Way We Were'. Rebecca made the introductions and I sat down nervously, almost dumbstruck. Mrs Lauder had broken her arm, and she was wearing an Hermès scarf as a sling.

The high tea arrived, and I helped Mrs Lauder to arrange some tiny scones with jam and cream on her plate. She was rather frail, certainly, but vibrant. She suddenly turned to me and said, 'Here, here. You need some more lipstick.' She reached into her handbag, pulled out a red lipstick and applied it to my lips. 'Yeah, I like that colour on you better,' she said in her strong New Yorker accent, satisfied. I had to agree it was, in fact, an improvement. Apparently it was an old trick from when she first started out selling cosmetics on the department store floor, and she still loved doing it. She was fabulous, and had a great sense of humour, so I recounted to her my own Estée Lauder anecdote.

I had always worn Youth Dew perfume, a particularly strong and spicy Lauder scent. A previous boyfriend had loved the way it smelt on me. He then dumped me for another woman and I was devastated. He had the nerve to call a few weeks later. I thought he was ringing to confess he'd made a dreadful mistake in leaving me, but he just wanted me to return a navy-blue cashmere overcoat he had left at my house. Sobbing, I poured an entire bottle of Youth Dew Bath Oil over the lining of the coat, because that stuff is so pungent no amount of dry-cleaning would ever, ever remove the smell. Thankfully I don't think I came off as too much of a bunny boiler because Mrs Lauder and Rebecca laughed at my story. I still can't visit New York and not make a mental connection to Mrs Lauder and that wonderful company. To me, they are inseparable.

Not long afterwards the Lauder group extended a surprise invitation to *Vogue Australia* to attend the launch of new skincare treatment,

Fruition, in the UK two days later. I had no idea what awaited; I had been given no itinerary.

I was collected at Heathrow by a uniformed chauffeur who bundled me into a sparkling new Bentley and delivered me to the astonishingly grand Cliveden House country hotel in Berkshire, a rendezvous favoured by the rich and powerful for over three hundred years. It was also the backdrop for the John Profumo/Christine Keeler political scandal in the early sixties. I couldn't wait to see the pool house which had played a starring role in that story. As I was checking in, I was informed that since I had come further than any other journalist I had been given the Lady Astor Suite. This tyranny of distance would ironically prove to be a great bonus for many years to come. I was always kindly given the best room in the house because of the kilometres travelled. Little did anyone know, the long haul flight from Australia to anywhere has never bothered me, and in fact I find it quite relaxing. I have always refused to suffer from jet lag in order to not miss out on any potential experience waiting on the other side. Surely you can talk yourself out of being tired if the option that night is a glittering formal dinner by the fireplace in the Great Hall, which, as it happened, was the plan for the evening.

The palatial Lady Astor Suite afforded a sweeping view of the manicured gardens. As I threw open the huge doors and stepped onto the terrace, I noticed gardeners below atop spindly wooden ladders, clipping topiary trees into precise formations. After showering and changing, I rushed down the great staircase and outside, enjoying the crunch of gravel under my boots. A late afternoon fog had crept in and was curling around the trees. I nodded hello to one of the gardeners and in my imagination he doffed his tweed cap and said 'Good evening, Milady'. I was in heaven. Pity I hadn't packed any DH

Lawrence novels. And to think, thirty hours before I'd been in a fluoro-lit office in Greenwich, Sydney, writing captions.

Perhaps I indulged my passion for the Gothic a little too much because when I returned to my suite after an abundant dinner, I became convinced there was a ghost in my room. I swear the cold tap in the bathroom turned itself on noisily twice during the night. I spent the night sitting up in bed with the bedclothes clutched around my shoulders, terrified, but thankfully the night cream I had been gifted was some comfort. These things tend to cancel each other out.

I will never forget the time when in another gesture of extreme generosity, Shiseido invited Karin and me to travel together to Japan to better understand the breadth of their phenomenal business. Apart from the many cosmetic and toiletry brands in the group, Shiseido also has investments in fine dining restaurants, especially French. As it transpired Karin, who was always a finicky eater anyway, had just fallen pregnant with her first child. Understandably, she did not want to eat raw food or anything too exotic, as she was feeling slightly queasy. But our strictly planned itinerary had us booked in to eat at the top fine dining restaurants in Tokyo, both Japanese and French. Every meal, lunch and dinner alike, was a ten-course degustation menu at the very least, containing smoke, foam and random slimy surprises from under the sea. The Japanese are the most gracious and attentive hosts in the world, but the combination of tradition, propriety and a rigid timetable meant there was no room for, 'Could we please just skip it and order some fries?'

Poor Karin couldn't eat a bite. Not wanting to offend as guests, but understanding that she was feeling bilious at the mere idea of coddled sea urchin, I ate for Australia, to cover up the fact that Karin was eating nothing. It put me off degustation for life. For all my years as a

Vogue editor clients assumed I was a foodie, but I'm really much happier with a chop and some spinach.

I hoovered my way through four days of non-stop, I'm-not-quite-sure-what food and wine in Tokyo, until we ended up in the incredible Kimono Museum in Kyoto. After being draped with layer upon layer of antique ceremonial kimonos, accessorised with a fetching obi, I regarded myself in the mirror and discovered I was a not dissimilar size to Mount Fuji.

On another occasion, Shiseido organised a launch in Penang, Malaysia, a somewhat inexplicable destination for a beauty launch given the almost unbearable humidity. A number of beauty journalists were sent to spend time with the creative director and master perfumer Serge Lutens, an impenetrable Frenchman who can't—or won't—speak English and loathes interviews: always a challenge. He also refused to take off his super-snug, black wool suit, so all I recall from the experience is perspiration (him), frizzy hair (me), and the realisation I'd have to craft something really clever to produce a good story.

In today's environment, there is so much more working against the journalist who is trying to do a good job. Many cosmetic and fashion companies are attempting to eliminate the journalist entirely anyway, by offering what they call 'master interviews' with the talent, be it a perfume 'nose', celebrity face or makeup artist. These Q and A's have been prepared by the PR department, who devise all the questions themselves with the sole purpose of delivering the company message. To me, this is the antithesis of what a creative publishing title stands for, but the pressure was certainly there—the implication from the client being that if they allow you to print it first, it's somehow an 'exclusive'.

I put a ban on master interviews under my editorship. Your reader deserves better than that. The day you accept a master interview and a 'hand out' shot from the client, which is normally an 'exclusive' behind-the-scenes photograph from the advertising shoot, I think you may as well shut up shop, but unfortunately this is the way the industry is heading. Email interviews are also questionable, as you can't be sure who the person at the other end answering them is. We learnt this the hard way when we were offered an exclusive opportunity to send some questions to the actress Elizabeth Taylor. We received her replies and took it in good faith that she had answered them, but a reader spotted a quote he had read before and called *Media Watch*. It was a marvellous chance for them to put the words '*Vogue*' and 'Elizabeth Taylor' together to get a ratings boost, especially when Ms Taylor herself telephoned and left a message on their answering machine saying she had indeed answered our questions personally. That was a gift for *Media Watch*. They even broadcast her words on the radio to promote the show. Despite the fact that they dragged my writer and me through the mire with their sanctimonious outrage, I was thrilled to the core to find an apology from Ms Taylor on my phone. *The* Elizabeth Taylor. It made my year.

A highlight of the Penang trip was meeting Deborah Thomas, who was the then deputy of *Cleo* magazine. She and I decided to make a shopping stopover in Bangkok on the way home, bonded over dinner at The Peninsula Hotel, and have been wonderful friends ever since. Deborah has had a long and stellar career at Australian Consolidated Press, and has edited numerous magazines in that stable over the years, including *Cleo*, *Elle*, *Mode* and *The Australian Women's Weekly*. She is a total pro. When Deb was the deputy at *Cleo*, and Lisa Wilkinson was the editor, they produced, in my opinion, the best women's lifestyle magazine this country has ever had. The energy and enthusiasm leapt off every page. They understood, respected and genuinely identified with their readers.

* * *

Being the beauty editor at *Vogue* meant I was constantly meeting and working with the world's top models. When Claudia Schiffer was at the height of her fame, she came to Sydney on a promotional tour for Revlon. My great friend Janet Muggivan, who has been the PR for Revlon for forever, was in charge of taking care of Claudia for the duration of her stay. I called Janet to ask what Claudia looked like in the flesh. 'Oh you know,' she said monotone. 'Tall. Perfect skin. Baby face. Masses of blonde hair. Body of a goddess. Your basic nightmare.'

There was an ultra-VIP function for Claudia later that week, and loads of us were transferred over to Fort Denison in Sydney Harbour where a type of giant bamboo hut had been erected. I think a balmy tropical evening was anticipated but—as is usual when you plan a summer party—there were ferocious winds and lashing rain. The water taxis on the journey over were lurching from side to side on the waves that had been whipped up by the weather. You practically needed storm gear.

The 'hut' was packed to capacity and some clever event planner had placed candelabras everywhere, the live flames licking not very far from the straw roof. I had to be saved by firemen from a burning apartment building once in my early twenties because I panicked, and ever since then I have had a morbid habit of obsessively checking fire exits. I know where the fire exit is in every hotel I stay in. I'm also quite claustrophobic. I always evaluate the exits in fashion shows, and if it doesn't look like there are enough I leave, because there's no way in hell that crowd is going to leave their handbags, stay calm and go in single file. When it comes to the fashion set, panic is always the new black.

Claudia finally arrived. This we knew because although you couldn't see her in the crush of bodies, her entrance was heralded by a regal blast of trumpets and everybody going crazy. It was about then I started hyperventilating and thinking: 'We're all going to die, die, die.'

I recall manoeuvering myself in the direction of a plastic exit flap, a position that would allow me to squeeze out before everyone else and step onto the wall of the fort. From there, it would be a daring jump into the chill water, after which I could take my chances swimming to shore with the sharks. 'Fire & Ice baby, it's Revlon heritage,' Janet said drily when I recounted my panic attack to her later.

As a rule though, planning a quick and painless getaway from a celebrity launch is crucial. The last time I felt terror like that was when I was trapped several years ago in the Dolce & Gabbana boutique in Milan when Victoria Beckham was the star guest. I don't want to spend my last moments on earth being crushed to death by overdressed fashionistas taking photos on their iPhones.

* * *

There were many noteworthy editorial successes during the years Nancy was editor. Annita Keating, wife of the then prime minister Paul Keating, agreed to appear in a six-page spread in the magazine, and was also game enough for a glamorous makeover. In what we now refer to as 'The Great Hair Straightening Incident of 1993', Mrs Keating's trademark long curls were blow-dried straight. The resultant photographs were chic and elegant and created a storm of controversy in the press, probably due to the fact that no one had ever seen an Australian first lady look quite so fabulous. Mrs Keating came into the fashion office to select and try on clothes, and everybody was terribly nervous at the idea of fitting the wife of the prime minister, but she was very receptive and friendly. *Vogue Australia* has never covered a first lady since then, although we did have a stand-by position on Susie Annus when Kim Beazley was the Opposition Leader. We did not approach Julia Gillard when she became prime minister as it stood to reason that starring in *Vogue* with earrings by Cartier may not have been a major priority. As it turns out, Ms Gillard featured in a wonderful and much more appropriate spread in *The Australian Women's Weekly*, styled brilliantly by, as it turns out, Judith Cook.

It was a few months later in 1993 that Nancy came to my desk with some photographs that had been sent to her by photographer Grant Good, who had spotted a beautiful seventeen-year-old Aboriginal girl at Dreamworld on the Gold Coast called Elaine George. It was immediately arranged that the pair should fly down to shoot a cover for the September issue. While it did happen to coincide with the International Year of the World's Indigenous People, it was not a cynical exercise for publicity. Elaine was a true beauty and had been genuinely 'discovered', Hollywood-style. The cover was a huge success, although we did receive some backlash that she did not look 'Aboriginal' enough. The fact is that Elaine is quite light-skinned and the cover lighting was blown out, but apparently she received criticism from her elders for the same reason.

Vogue Australia was very prepared to champion and mentor Elaine's burgeoning career, but she was a shy, self-effacing girl who did not like the attention or the limelight. Nancy and I were getting her dressed one day for an on-stage appearance to publicise her cover. The dress we had chosen was a sort of Grecian-inspired dress of crushed silk, but we noticed that Elaine seemed uncomfortable. Nancy asked her if she didn't like the dress. Elaine replied that she liked it very much, it was just that her mother had told her never to wear something that looked wrinkled and unironed. She was so sweet. Elaine, and her agent, sensibly decided that modelling was not the career for her, but she set a stellar precedent for Indigenous models. The next time we featured an Aboriginal model on the cover was Samantha Harris in June 2010.

Sam is another quiet, unassuming girl, and I think one of the most beautiful models this country has ever produced. Happily, her issue sold like crazy too. Australian readers are very supportive of the local girls. Sam was wearing a bright-yellow, cut-away Pucci gown on her cover, and I later received a handwritten note from the designer Peter Dundas, who wrote: 'Thank you for the amazing cover. You really, really get who the Pucci girl is!' How wonderful that the Pucci girl is also proudly Aboriginal.

In 1994, Nancy invited director Baz Luhrmann and his creative partners, production designer Catherine Martin and graphic designer Bill Marron, to be the first ever guest editors of *Vogue Australia*. The team had recently won great acclaim with the film *Strictly Ballroom*, and the idea of engaging them to produce a magazine was visionary.

The issue featured a stunning series of old-Hollywood-style black-and-white portraits of Nicole Kidman channelling various famous actresses, shot by Rocky Schenk in LA, and a *Life* magazine-inspired portfolio of Kylie Minogue, based on *A Star is Born* and shot by photography great Bert Stern (who shot the famous 'Last Sitting' with Marilyn Monroe). There was also a camp, fifties pin-up-style shoot called 'Calendar Girls', shot by Grant Matthews, featuring Tara Morice, Deni Hines and the incomparable Magda Szubanski, among others. My job was to interview them all and then write cheesy extended captions, a task I relished.

Beauty was to change my life in another way, not just on a career level. In 1992 I was flown to Paris, again by Shiseido, to attend and cover the launch of a new fragrance by Serge Lutens: Féminité du bois (still one of my favourite scents). After business was finished I arranged to stay on for a couple of days with a model friend, a crazy Texan called Deanna. Models are very good friends to have. Being dazzlingly beautiful, they are invited everywhere, get into every cool club and get all the best tables. They also attract men who like models (bad) and other men who are really nice but too intimidated to talk to them, so they talk to the model's girlfriends—like me—instead (good). Wayne's girlfriend back on the Gold Coast had the wrong end of the stick entirely. Beautiful people improve life enormously.

Deanna was, as might be expected, hanging out with the band Guns N' Roses, who were touring. Thus I ended up backstage watching them perform at a giant stadium on the outskirts of Paris, along with some leather-clad supermodels. After the show, I found myself in a nightclub trying in vain to think of something to say to a very bored Slash, the guitarist, when it suddenly struck me as all too hard, and best left to the models who may have even cared about what he said in reply.

The following night I was having dinner at a bistro with Charla Carter, *Vogue Australia*'s Paris-based editor; a chic, crazy Californian who has become a very dear friend and long-time colleague. She suggested we go for a drink at Le Casbah, the then hottest nightclub in Paris, so we walked the few blocks to the club behind la Bastille and ordered champagne.

Around midnight, Charla and her husband excused themselves and left. By this time I had been joined by some mad friends from Sydney, one being a six-foot-four Lebanese drag queen, who was in all her full-blown, full-length finery, and we were having a ball. I was due to fly home to Australia the next morning, however, so made a move to leave at around 2 a.m. I marched up to a tall, dark and exotic-looking doorman called Mourad and asked him to call me a taxi. He decided I needed another champagne instead. He and I then went on a whirlwind, super-VIP tour of every top club in Paris, ending up at Folies Pigalle sitting in a booth with Michael Hutchence at 6 a.m.

Despite the huge night, I made it onto my flight the next morning, and when I arrived back in Sydney I discovered a very romantic message on my answering machine in French. Mourad wanted to fly me back so we could summer together in Marrakech.

I knew who would enjoy that story. I rushed into Judith's office and told her. 'Judith, an extremely sexy man I've known for six hours wants to fly me to Marrakech!'

'You have to wear jewel-coloured silk pyjamas, say ruby or emerald, and paint your nails dark red!' she said dramatically. 'And your luggage needs to have striped lining!' It was a typically *Vogue* suggestion, one that completely bypassed the rational and leapt straight to the exciting.

Nancy was a little more realistic. We talked about the possibility that he may be a serial killer and that if I needed an airfare home, she would wire me the money. I thought he had been too cool and well-connected to be a murderer, and when I disembarked at Charles de Gaulle airport a few weeks later and saw him in his black leather Perfecto jacket and Timberland boots, dragging on a Marlboro, I knew I'd made a good decision. Two years later, I would move to Paris.

4

MODEL BEHAVIOUR

One of the most controversial aspects of fashion magazines, and the fashion industry, is models. Specifically, how young they are and how thin they are. It's a topic that continues to create endless debates, in the press and in the community. As the editor of *Vogue*, my opinion was constantly sought on these issues, and the images we produced in the magazine were closely scrutinised. It's a precarious subject, and there are many unpleasant truths beneath the surface that are not discussed or acknowledged publicly.

When I first began dealing with models in the late eighties we were generally drawing from a pool of local beauties. These girls were naturally willowy and slim, had glowing skin, shiny hair and loads of energy. They ate lunch, sparingly for sure, but they ate. They were not skin and bones. I don't think anyone believes that a model can eat anything she wants, not exercise and still stay a flawless size 8 (except when they are very young), so whatever regime these girls were following was keeping them healthy.

But I began to recognise the signs that other models were using different methods to stay svelte. I was dressing a model from the US on a beauty shoot, and I noticed scars and scabs on her knees. When I queried her about them she said nonchalantly: 'Oh, yes. Because I'm always so hungry, I faint a lot.' She thought it was completely normal to pass out every day, sometimes more than once.

On another shoot I was chatting to one of the top Australian girls over lunch. She had just moved to Paris, and was sharing a small apartment with another model. I asked her how that was working out. 'I get a lot of time by myself actually,' she said, picking at her salad. 'My flatmate is a "fit model", so she's in hospital on a drip a lot of the time.' A fit model is one who is used in the top designer ateliers, or workrooms, and is the body around which the clothes are designed. That the ideal body shape used as a starting point for a collection should be a female on the brink of hospitalisation from starvation is frightening.

The longer I worked with models, the more the food deprivation became obvious. Cigarettes and Diet Coke were dietary staples. Sometimes you would see the tell-tale signs of anorexia, where a girl develops a light fuzz on her face and arms as her body struggles to stay warm. I have never, ever, in all my career, heard a model say 'I'm hot', not even if you wrapped her in fur and put her in the middle of the Kimberley Desert.

Society is understandably concerned about the issues surrounding body image and eating disorders, and the dangerous and unrealistic messages being sent to young women via fashion journals. When it comes to who should be blamed for the portrayal of overly thin models, magazine editors are in the direct line of fire, but the conundrum is more complex. The 'fit model' begins the fashion process: designer outfits are created around a live, in-house skeleton. Very few designers have a curvy or petite fit model. These collections are then sent to the runway, worn by tall, pin-thin models because that's the way the designer wants to see the clothes fall. There will also be various casting directors and stylists involved, who have a vision of the type of women they envisage wearing these clothes. For some bizarre reason, it seems they prefer her to be young, coltish, six-foot tall and built like a prepubescent boy.

It is too simplistic to blame misogynistic men, although in some cases I believe that criticism is deserved. There are a few male fashion designers I would like to personally strangle. But there are many female fashion editors who perpetuate the stereotype, women who often have a major eating disorder of their own. They get so caught up in the hype of how brilliant clothes look on a size 4 they cannot see the inherent danger in the message. It cannot be denied that visually, clothes fall better on a slimmer frame, but there is slim, and then there is scary skinny.

Despite protestations by women who recognise the danger of portraying any one body type as 'perfect', the situation is not improving. If you look back at the heady days of the supermodels in the late eighties and early nineties, beauties such as Cindy Crawford, Eva Herzigová and Claudia Schiffer look positively curvaceous compared to the sylphs of today. There was a period in the last three years when some of the girls on the runways were so young and thin, and the shoes they were modelling so high, it actually started to seem barbaric to me. I would watch the ready-to-wear shows on the edge of my seat, apprehensive and anxious. I'm not comfortable witnessing teen waifs on almost the literal point of collapse.

After the shows, the collection is made available for the press to use for their shoots. These are the samples we all work with and they are obviously the size of the model who wore them on the runway. Thus, a stylist must cast a model who will fit into these tiny sizes. And they have become smaller since the early noughties. We've had couture dresses arrive from Europe that are so miniscule they resemble christening robes. There are no bigger samples available, and in any case, the designer probably has no interest in seeing their clothes on larger women. Many high fashion labels are aghast at the idea of producing a size 14, and they certainly wouldn't want to see it displayed in the pages of the glossies. As a *Vogue* editor I was of the opinion that we didn't necessarily need to feature size 14-plus models in every issue. It is a fashion magazine; we are showcasing the clothes. I am of the belief that an intelligent reader understands that a model is chosen because she carries clothes well. Some fashion would suit a curvier girl, some wouldn't. I see no problem with presenting a healthy, toned, size Australian 10. But as sample sizes from the runway shows became smaller and smaller, 10 was no longer an option and the girls were dieting drastically to stay in the game.

It is the ultimate vicious cycle. A model who puts on a few kilos can't get into a sample size on a casting and gets reprimanded by her agency. She begins to diet, loses the weight, and is praised by all for how good she looks. But instead of staying at that weight, and trying to maintain it through sensible diet and exercise, she thinks losing more will make her even more desirable. And no one tells her to stop.

Girls who can't diet their breasts away will have surgical reductions. They then enter into dangerous patterns of behaviour that the industry—shockingly—begins to accept as par for the course. We had a term for this spiral in the office. When a model who was getting good work in Australia starved herself down two sizes in order to be cast in the overseas shows—one of the ultimate achievements for models, and the first step to an international career—the *Vogue* fashion office would say she'd become 'Paris thin'. This dubious achievement was generally accompanied by mood swings, extreme fatigue, binge eating and sometimes bouts of self-harming. All in the quest to fit into a Balenciaga sample.

Not every model has an eating disorder, but I would suggest that every model is not eating as much as she would like to. In 1995 I cast a lovely Russian model for a studio shoot in Paris, and I noticed that by mid-afternoon she hadn't eaten a thing (we always catered). Her energy was fading, so I suggested we stop so she could have a snack. She shook her head and replied, 'No, no. It is my job not to eat.' It was one of the only sentences she knew how to say in English.

A few years later we booked another Russian girl, who also was starving herself, on a trip to Marrakech. When the team went out to dinner at night she ordered nothing, but then hunger would get the better of her and she would pick small pieces of food off other people's plates. I've seen it happen on many trips. The models somehow rationalise that if they didn't order anything, then they didn't really take in the kilojoules. They can tell their booker at the agency before they sleep that they only had a salad. By the end of the trip, she didn't have the energy to even sit up; she could barely open her eyes. We actually had her lie down next to a fountain to get the last shot. Naomi telephoned her agency to report that we thought she had a serious eating disorder, but we got the 'No, it's just that she hasn't been well lately' spiel.

In 2004, a fashion season where the girls were expected to be particularly bone-thin, I was having lunch in New York with a top model agent who confidentially expressed her concern to me, as she did not want to be the one to expose the conspiracy. 'It's getting very serious,' she said. She lowered her tone and glanced around to see if anyone at the nearby tables could hear. 'The top casting directors are demanding that they be thinner and thinner. I've got about four girls in hospital. And a couple of the others have resorted to eating tissues. Apparently they swell up and fill your stomach.'

As a not unintelligent woman, I was horrified to hear what the industry was covering up and I felt complicit. We were all complicit. But in my experience it is practically impossible to get a photographer or a fashion editor—male or female—to acknowledge the repercussions of using very thin girls. They don't want to. For them, it's all about the drama of the photograph. They convince themselves that the girls are just genetically blessed, or have achieved it through energetic bouts of yoga and some goji berries.

I was at the baggage carousel with a fashion editor collecting our luggage after a trip and I noticed an extremely anorexic woman standing nearby. She was the most painfully thin person I had ever seen, and my heart went out to her. I pointed her out to the editor who scrutinised the poor woman and said: 'I know it sounds terrible but I think she looks really great.' The industry is rife with this level of body dysmorphia from mature women.

This was really hammered home to me when there was a swimsuit casting at the *Vogue* office in the late nineties. After seeing dozens of top girls, the then fashion editor decided that not one of them had the 'perfect' body. The *Vogue* office was situated across the road from the Northside Clinic, which specialises in treating eating disorders. The Clinic also happened to house the only café near the office. I walked over to buy a fat-free chicken sandwich after the casting had wrapped up, and regarded the pale, young, female patients on portable IV drips, smoking in the courtyard in their dressing gowns. The sad irony did not escape me that none of the gorgeous models we had seen that day had been considered suitable to wear a bikini in *Vogue*.

In my early years at the magazine there was no minimum age limit on models, and there were certainly occasions that girls under the age of sixteen were used. Fourteen-year-old beauty Kristy Hinze graced the January 1995 cover and was instantly put under contract with *Vogue*. Kristy had a fresh, outdoorsy appeal, bright-green eyes and a beaming smile. The fashion team tended to feature her frolicking at the beach, or staring serenely into the camera next to a horse: she had an Aussie glamour that was also wholesome.

The readers had no complaint about her age, because she wasn't being dressed up to look more mature, or overtly sexy. Sexiness in the early days of *Vogue Australia* was more equated with the sun and surf than playing a vamp. Younger girls can also differ wildly in terms of maturity.

For one job, I had to collect two models from the airport: one a fifteen-year-old brunette from Melbourne who had never flown interstate, and the other a sixteen-year-old from Germany. The Melbourne girl arrived, wide-eyed and terribly shy, practically clinging to me for the whole shoot. The other girl was a gum-snapping, chain-smoking sexpot, who arrived with her fifty-year-old boyfriend. I don't recall either of the shoots being terribly successful.

Over time, readers did become more critical of models who looked too young and too thin, perhaps in direct correlation to how much the industry was using them. When you receive a well-written letter from a polite and astute reader asking why you are choosing children to promote fashion for women, it is difficult to respond with any level of intelligence. It is a legitimate question.

In 2005 I was on a location trip to Morocco with my fashion editor Naomi, waiting for a model—a new face predicted to have a big future—to arrive from Paris. Her plane had been delayed and as she was not going to make it to the hotel until very late, we went to bed. When we went to the model's room the next morning, we found her in bed sleepy-faced and clutching a large teddy bear. She looked about twelve years old. I was horrified.

Under my editorship the fashion office found a new favourite model—Katie Braatvedt, a fifteen-year-old from New Zealand. Katie would travel to Sydney for shoots, always accompanied by her mother who was a priest. On one shoot, I sat and chatted with her mother, while she wrote next Sunday's sermon.

Katie was indeed gorgeous and we had her under contract: the idea being that *Vogue* grooms and protects the girls at the beginning of their careers. But in April 2007 I ran a cover of Katie wearing an Alex Perry gown and standing in a treehouse, and received a storm of protest, from readers and the media, accusing us of sexualising children. I lamely debated the point that this was not the message we intended, and that the photographs were meant to be innocent and enchanting, until I decided to give up. I was being led by what the fashion office wanted, not what the reader wanted.

This is a constant tension when you are an editor. In the end I had to agree wholeheartedly with the readers. How had *Vogue*'s viewpoint become so narrow that we had to fly in a fifteen-year-old from New Zealand every time we shot? Was there not a broader range of beauty that we could celebrate? I felt foolish even trying to justify it. What do you say: 'Oh, but she's pretty'?

I immediately instigated a policy that we would not employ models under the age of sixteen. If a girl under sixteen was discovered who had potential, we kept an eye on her and had her agency update us with new photos every six months or so. I don't think it would be a bad idea to push the age limit up to eighteen. Fifteen- and sixteen-year-olds tend to be naturally slim, but at eighteen or nineteen years bodies begin to mature and change. Would it not be preferable to start a career with a slightly more womanly body, rather than fall into the trap of starving yourself back to your sixteen-year-old shape?

Sales remained steady on the magazine, so clearly my decision to ban girls under the age of sixteen had no negative repercussions. *Vogue* internationally has since launched a project in June 2012 called the Health Initiative, instigated by US *Vogue* editor-in-chief Anna Wintour, which bans the use of models under sixteen and pledges that they will not use models they know to be suffering from eating disorders. The first part you can police. The second is disingenuous nonsense, because unless you are monitoring their diet 24/7, you just can't be sure.

In 2011, I was sent an email from a US agency informing me that 'plus-size' model Robyn Lawley was returning to Australia and that *Vogue* may be interested in seeing her. When I opened the attachment I discovered Robyn was drop-dead gorgeous, with a beautiful face and great legs. 'Plus-size' meant she was about a size 14 around the bosom and hips. I was sure the reader would appreciate seeing this glamorous girl who was slightly more representative of your average woman. The fashion department, however, were a little harder to persuade.

I got the usual protestations about how there would be no samples in a size 14 and what kind of fashion would they put on a plus-size model anyway? I left them to work it out, determined to push the story through. Fashion editor Meg Gray took it on, and created a lovely narrative that celebrated Robyn's curves, using pencil skirts and blouses and snug black evening dresses. When I went to the studio to watch the shoot most of the men in the room couldn't concentrate, she looked so sexy. Robyn's manager, Chelsea Bonner from Bella Models, arrived, as it was a proud day for her agency. Her first 'plus-sized' girl in *Vogue Australia*.

'You know,' I said to Chelsea, as we watched Robyn expertly go through her poses, 'I don't actually see her as plus-sized at all. She's just beautiful.' The issue was a resounding success with readers, and garnered more press than I expected.

Robyn and I were both booked to appear on the *Sunrise* programme to talk about the shoot. Robyn was in New York and linked via video. After she very graciously commented about how exciting it was to appear in *Vogue*, host David Koch turned to me—rather crankily I thought—and said: 'But she's not really plus-sized is she? She's normal size.' And I agreed. The high fashion world has a deep vein of callousness. For every woman who related to the lovely photographs of a curvaceous Robyn, there is a stylist in Paris eating iceberg lettuce hearts sprayed with Evian for lunch and telling the hopeful young models they are too fat to get into the jacket.

5

THE PARIS YEARS

Paris had put a spell on me, as it does to so many people. From the time I met my future husband Mourad in 1992, I had so many trips back and forth for work we managed to keep a long-distance relationship going for two years. It was probably helped enormously by the fact that neither of us spoke much of each other's language, so while it was easy to sometimes get exasperated, it was difficult to argue.

I was approaching my ten-year long service at *Vogue*. In a grand romantic gesture, I resigned from my job as beauty editor. I was going to move to Paris, live a bohemian and glamorous life, and write. Surely I was the first journalist in the world who had ever thought of this, *non*? I had no savings. I had no French. I had no papers. I had no clue.

Fortunately, I was surrounded by more practical people who did. While still in Sydney I moved in with my friend Deborah Thomas, saving on rent to try to build up my bank balance. Deborah was the editor of *Mode* at the time. We would share a bottle of wine at night, while she worked on her magazine grid and I read all the trash magazines she brought home from the office.

Vogue's publisher Lesley Wild was on good terms with the French Consul General and managed to help me secure both an appointment and the requisite visa. Editor Nancy Pilcher, who never stopped helping me throughout my career, agreed that I could contribute stories from Paris. It is gratifying to remember how supportive my colleagues were in those days. Everyone had your back, as opposed to stabbing you in it.

I was determined to find my own apartment in Paris, and not immediately move in with Mourad, who seemed reasonably nonchalant about me relocating there anyway. I didn't want the relationship to be the sole basis of my decision—if things didn't work out with him then no problem, I would still have my independence.

The *Vogue* team threw a farewell party in the boardroom and I was handed a card and present. We had a 'little blue box' tradition, which meant that any gift for a staff member always came from Tiffany. My package, however, revealed two sets of Yves Saint Laurent lingerie and a cookbook, which were the perfect send off for a Gallic romance.

In reality, I should have asked for a fax machine.

* * *

It was 1994 and I was living in my first Paris home, a tiny one-bedroom apartment on the Rue Rameau, in the busy 2nd arrondissement. It was seven flights up a steep circular stairway, with no elevator. The mere act of collecting the mail every day was arduous, but in three months I dropped a dress size. I was probably about an size Australian 12, if that, when I arrived in Paris, but I immediately felt hefty compared to the sparrow-thin French girls. The tables and chairs were always so close in the cafés; I felt conspicuous and ungainly.

Shopping one day, I walked into the Miu Miu boutique in the Rue de Grenelle and timidly asked the sales assistant if she had a particular coat that was in the window in my size. She stared at me stony-faced, took a deep drag on her cigarette (they smoked in the shops then), blew it out through her nose and said: 'No, there is nothing in this store that would fit you.' I left, mortified.

I had promised myself when I settled in Paris that I would avoid the patisseries, except for bread and croissants. I do not have a sweet tooth at any rate so it was not difficult. That was my only dietary taboo, and by the end of the year I was the slimmest I have ever been. I put it all down to walking. Perhaps that's why French women don't get fat, because they all walk everywhere. For me, every single square centimetre of Paris was enthralling. I covered tens of kilometres on foot every day. Sadly, I don't get the same frisson of excitement now when I walk from my house to Bondi Junction mall.

That first year in Paris was one of the best years of my life. Because I could not yet speak the language, I spent an enormous amount of time in my own thoughts, just observing. I read a book each day and explored the city, with no specific destinations planned. I was mostly alone, but never lonely. At night I lived a crazy nightclub existence with Mourad. I called him Le Vampire because he never saw full daylight, going to bed at 8 a.m. and getting up at 4 p.m.

Le Casbah was the top club in Paris, and Mourad was the man you needed to know to get in. Everywhere we went, the doors opened, tables were miraculously found, champagne was sent out; he would toss his keys to someone and they would park his car. He ripped up his parking tickets. He didn't have to settle restaurant bills. He knew every policeman. It was intoxicating. It was like I had been dropped into the film *Goodfellas*, although it needed English subtitles. I couldn't understand a word anyone was saying, especially at 4 a.m. in Les Bain Douches, but everything sounded sexy and thrilling. No doubt it was just the regular alcohol- and drug-fuelled rubbish people say in nightclubs in the early hours of the morning, but in my head, Jean Paul Sartre and Anaïs Nin would have struggled to keep up.

In general, our regime was to wake up in the late afternoon, have something resembling a brunch at a local bistro in the lesbian district in the 2nd, visit three or four nightclubs, and usually end up at a smoky, windowless, red-velvet bar called Babylone in Les Halles, at 7 a.m., eating *steak frites* with the African musicians who had just finished their gigs at various venues around town. Every night we mingled with celebrities, aristocrats, artists, drag queens, designers and criminals; it was fabulous.

There were various talented Aussie expatriates living in Paris at that period: Christina Zimpel, the previous art director of *Vogue Australia*, and her husband Patric Shaw, who had turned to photography, and writer Lee Tulloch and her photographer husband Tony Amos. Lee, Tony and their daughter Lolita lived in the most beautiful apartment near the Sorbonne, and would often invite me over for a home-cooked dinner. Some of my most delightful recollections of that time in Paris were sitting with Lee in cafés for hours and hours, talking about the books we were reading, or in her case, writing. Lee was contributing to *Elle Australia*, under the editorship of Deborah

Thomas who had moved from *Mode*, while I had been hired to be the beauty editor and editor-at-large for *Vogue Singapore*, which had launched in 1994. Lee, who had seen great success with her first novel *Fabulous Nobodies*, was writing her second book *Wraith*.

Needless to say Paris was an endless source of possibilities for a fashion and beauty journalist. For the first time in my career I was attending the ready-to-wear (RTW) shows. I would later work under many managers who never fully appreciated the importance of the RTW to a fashion journalist. The shows, to a purely financial person, appeared to be an indulgent waste of money. It is impossible to explain to someone who is fixated on reducing costs that the international shows deliver inspiration and expertise, giving an editor a sense of context, history and insider knowledge. By experiencing the moments, you can make comparisons and draw conclusions. You meet the players; you are a legitimate part of the game. But the RTW show season was pretty much viewed by Australian management as editors and writers taking an overseas holiday. I have had to write a lengthy justification explaining why I thought it was necessary to attend each RTW season, twice a year for the last decade.

I need to clarify that I have never been completely obsessed with fashion. I am fascinated by popular culture, and fashion is of course one of its most important informants and signifiers. But the couture shows, which I was now excitingly attending in Paris, gave me a whole new appreciation. The shows were very intimate, and reserved for only top-shelf press and customers. Couture is by its very nature a luxury, and only very select journalists were in attendance. Working for *Vogue Singapore* meant that I was automatically granted a front row seat, as opposed to either no seat or a standing seat for *Vogue*

Australia. It was not exactly snobbery, but if you don't have the couture customers, you don't get the chair. My colleagues and I used to call it the 'you're only as good as your economy' rule.

There were often two shows: the first for the press, the second exclusively for clients. Back then no one dressed up; no one took photos of each other outside wearing the latest Givenchy sweater. There were no 'It Girls', unless you count Bernadette Chirac. We all had notebooks and wrote or sketched each 'exit' (not my biggest strength, but Charla Carter's sketches were a work of art). We watched the show, as opposed to trying to be the show.

Although I was usually seated with the international press, I felt more like part of the French brigade because I was living there. I recall rushing to a Chanel show at the Hôtel Ritz, late, because there had been a problem with the Metro. I dashed through torrential rain and made it just in time to hurl myself into my tiny gilt chair. I looked down at my sodden ballet slippers, and was bunching my dripping everyday trench in my lap when I noticed I was seated right beside the impenetrable US *Vogue* editor-in-chief Anna Wintour. Reality would not have touched her Manolo Blahniks, but I didn't care about my wet feet. I was in heaven, living and working in Paris. And it was a very good seat.

If I was asked what the ultimate moment might be in the world of Paris high fashion, I would suggest that Christian Lacroix couture shows came very, very close. They were such an old-world, feminine experience, always held in grand ballrooms with the prerequisite spindly-gold chairs. His sense of fabrics, of clashing and combining colour, of texture and pattern, was extraordinary; each exit a work of art with a flamboyant nod to history and costume. A pink carnation was always placed across each chair, and when Lacroix appeared on the runway at the finale, guests would shower him with flowers, all accompanied by a soaring classical soundtrack. I'm not one to cry at fashion shows, but for some reason I often found his particularly moving and could find myself getting teary. For me, only the perfection of couture can produce that sort of emotion.

The appearance of a frail Yves Saint Laurent on the runway was also especially thrilling, not just for the beauty of his clothes. I felt an appreciation of the artist himself, his sensibilities, his innate taste, his love for the female form. He was Paris personified. Saint Laurent, creator of the iconic evening tuxedo 'Le Smoking'. What, to this day, could be more sexy? Actress Catherine Deneuve was almost always in the front row.

The great couturiers and their ateliers set a standard that is so remarkable, you feel transported when you see their vision come to life on the runway. Witness a Valentino couture show and you can imagine you are a princess at a dinner party in Rome in 1969. His collections were always so glossy, so expensive, so drop-dead chic. I was chatting to a British fashion journalist after one Valentino showing at the Louvre and she said grumpily: 'I thought all that was boring.' I can't begin to describe how badly dressed and ill-groomed the woman was. My response was a little more blunt. 'If you don't appreciate a Valentino couture show, then I don't think you should be working in fashion.'

One of the greatest advantages of working for *Vogue* is that it opens doors. Given that I was working across the areas of both beauty and fashion, I had access to the most amazing talents. On any given day I might be at a book launch with Italian designer Gianfranco Ferre choosing clothes to photograph at a designer showroom, interviewing the perfumer and 'nose' of Chanel, Jacques

Polge, or at a photographic shoot for a portrait of shoe designer Stephane Kelian.

In early 1995, Nancy contacted me and requested that I organise an interview and photoshoot with Tom Ford, a young American designing for Gucci who was creating waves in the industry. I dutifully began the arrangements, booking photographer Pascal Chevallier and newish model Diane Kruger, who is now an extremely successful Hollywood actress.

Ford was in the midst of preparing the Fall 1995 collection, so there were numerous phone calls and faxes back and forth with the Gucci PR office, trying to pin him down to a time. The whole process dragged on for weeks, and became so torturous Pascal called me at home one night and said, 'Really, *ca suffit*. Who does this Tom Ford think he is?' As it happened, the superb Fall 1995 collection, featuring skin-tight velvet hipsters, unbuttoned satin shirts and mohair coats, was a spectacular success that radically transformed the fortunes of the famed luxury house. Tom did, finally, arrive at the studio for our shoot, and immediately managed to charm the entire *Vogue* team. He is a dream to interview: extremely engaged, engaging and old-school polite. On the subsequent occasions that we met over the years, he always mentioned that shoot and told me that he regarded Pascal's portrait one of his favourite photographs ever taken. Ford went on to become so famous after our shoot it was impossible for an Australian publication to ever get access like that again, but I was fortunate to be in the right place at the right time. With the right editor.

Life wasn't a complete bed of roses in Paris. My retainer just stretched from week to week, the incessantly chilly weather took some getting used to, and there seemed to be a public transport strike weekly. My non-existent French became frustrating, never more so than when I applied for a *carte de residence* visa. Each time I visited the dreaded prefecture for one interview after the other, the tetchy staff would roll their eyes at my halting French. I knew enough to understand one woman when she hissed to her colleague: 'I don't know why these idiots want to live here when they can't even speak our language.' She did, I suppose, have a point, so I took to spending afternoons with Mourad's mother watching bad television.

For some inexplicable reason, the original *Dallas* and *Dynasty* series were still on-air in France, dubbed, and they are the perfect way to learn how to speak French fast. '*C'est pas vrai*!' ('It's not true!) 'How can you say that?' 'What do you think you are doing?!' Granted, the delivery may have been a little melodramatic, but it was thanks to those banal TV shows I learnt French 101.

Once I got the basics and knew how to marry, divorce and murder a man in French, I decided to enrol at the Alliance Francaise. I was happily ensconced in the middle of Course Two when I was surprised to discover that I was pregnant. '*C'est pas vrai*!' Mourad was thrilled. He had told me the first time we met that we would make beautiful babies, which was one of the major reasons I liked him in the first place.

My first visit to the obstetrician proved to be interesting. His English was worse than my French and after he had performed the ultrasound he said: 'The baby is good.' Then there was a pause and he continued staring at the screen. 'And the second baby is good.' I took it to mean, because of our jumbled Franglais, that the baby, the one baby, was really, really good. 'No,' he said haltingly. 'There are two babies.' I was having twins. Of course I was.

The first three months were a little tricky because—although I felt fine—I had the most heightened sense of smell, so using the Metro was impossible. The odours of Paris were too much. I could smell chewing gum stuck on the pavement one block away. With my supersensitive nose, I was like the character Grenouille in Patrick Susskind's novel *Perfume*. I would walk kilometres out of my way to avoid a cheese shop.

Walking on the Rue du Rivoli one steamy, hot lunchtime, I was so overcome by the smell of the traffic that I decided to duck into the WH Smith bookstore to breathe in the air conditioning. Once inside, I felt the nausea begin to overcome me, and I sort of slumped down next to the crime-novel section, pretending to read them, even though I was soon lying horizontal on the floor. A lovely Englishman came to my aid and said, 'You don't look so good. Shall I put you in a taxi?' He very kindly deposited me into a cab, which shortly pulled up outside my apartment block. As I walked gingerly to the door of the building, I had to pass the café outside and got a whiff of steak tartare. With the raw egg on the top. I promptly threw up in the street, on my Robert Clergerie sandals, in full view of the horrified patrons. It wasn't my finest moment in Paris, but from that day forward I felt absolutely brilliant.

My pregnancy did not slow my work, although I was so big people seemed a little nervous around me, thinking that I may be about to give birth any minute. My position as beauty editor of *Vogue Singapore* meant that I had to fly back and forth from Paris to Singapore quite regularly, but even at five months the airline officials were reluctant to let me on the plane, as it looked like labour was imminent.

I had decided that I wanted to give birth in Sydney so, six months pregnant, I flew back and moved in with my mother Gloria and her partner Robert. Mourad was to arrive just before my due date. For two weeks I caught up with friends, popped in and out of the *Vogue* offices and was having a generally marvellous time. Top of my list was to find an obstetrician and make all the necessary arrangements, but I was so busy I didn't quite get around to it. I did have a checkup at the local clinic and all was fine.

Nancy threw me the most lavish baby shower at The Observatory Hotel. I knew I was having boys, so everything was white and blue. The presents were beyond chic. It was a true *Vogue* pregnancy. Then, a few days after the celebration, as I sat at my mother's dining table typing out an invoice, my waters broke. I was only thirty-one weeks.

My mother was out, so I very calmly wrote her a note, which I left on the table, saying that I thought the babies were coming and I would call her later. I then rang my friend Janet, who—having no idea about having a baby whatsoever—suggested that I have a shower, and instructed me on what to wear and what to pack in my toiletries bag (well, she worked at Revlon).

I telephoned for a taxi, waited patiently, and when I got into the car asked the driver to take me to the nearest hospital. 'Are you going to have a baby?' he enquired, looking at me nervously. 'Yes,' was my response. 'Probably not right this second, but I can't be sure.' He drove like a demon, tossed me out into the driveway of Sutherland District Hospital and screeched away.

I trotted slowly into to the reception area. I thought I was handling myself with absolute aplomb, although Mum told me later that I had left the front door of the house wide open. 'Good afternoon,' I said politely to the woman on the desk. 'Ah. I'm pregnant. With twins. I'm only thirty-one weeks. And my waters just broke. I'm not registered here. Or with any doctor. And I'm not sure where my Medicare card is. My apologies.'

I will forever be one of Australia's greatest advocates of our health care system because I was immediately whisked to the labour ward and had the finest care anyone could be given, for what was a complicated premature delivery. It was necessary for the boys to be taken straight to special care and placed into humicribs, as they each weighed just under two kilos and were having difficulty breathing. My mother and my best friend from schooldays, Jenny, had both been with me in the labour ward, and I believe the experience put poor Jenny off having a baby for life.

I called Mourad in France, from my bed, letting him know his sons had arrived a little earlier than expected. Later that day I awoke in my own room, in the hospital I had been born in, knowing my babies were in safe hands. A magisterial kookaburra was sitting on the ledge of the balcony. It felt good to be home, if only for a while.

There were some truly *Vogue* moments during the fortnight I was in hospital. I was inundated with the most amazing flowers, from the best floral designers in Sydney, more and more, until my room resembled an enchanted garden. The nurses asked if they could bring people through to admire them, which was fine by me. My room became a popular tourist destination. You couldn't even find the twins among the foliage. And of course the beauty industry demonstrated their usual generosity and showered me with bounty. Displaying a classy understanding of what is truly important to a new mother after giving birth naturally to twins, Chanel sent the entire product line of Chanel No. 5. I distinctly recall shuffling down the hall in one of those regulation-issue hospital gowns, wheeling my drip and clutching a bottle of No. 5 Bath and Shower Gel.

Clinique delivered baby bibs and bottles in Clinique-green. The twins, named Joseph and Sam, were identical, and a handy tip I learnt from one of the floral sightseers was to paint the toenails of one baby, so you wouldn't mix them up and you would know who had just been fed. Once again, Chanel stepped in, supplying me with the popular

Rouge Noir nail lacquer, which I thought was a good, strong, masculine shade.

Three crazy months later I was back in Paris, thankfully with the most generous family-in-law that a new mother could ever wish for. Mourad's parents doted on their new grandsons, and were happy to take them overnight, often for days at a stretch. Mourad sometimes had to remind me to ask for them back.

We moved to a lovely apartment in Saint Germain en Laye, just outside of Paris, and while it was the end of my nightclubbing days our different schedules somehow seemed to work. I would spend the morning with the babies and then, when they went down for a sleep, call my editors in Singapore and Sydney to discuss upcoming stories. Mourad would then wake up, take over and I would head into the city and do interviews and shoots. Being based in Paris also meant that I could travel easily and so I did, incessantly, overnighting in Denmark to interview a scientist, weekending in London, attending the Biennale in Florence, or a lunch in Tuscany.

Quite the most extravagant beauty launch I was ever invited to attend during my time in Paris was held by Elizabeth Arden in 1994. It was a four day event and took place in Monte Carlo for the launch of a new fragrance, Sun Moon Stars, created by legendary designer Karl Lagerfeld. Most excitingly, my friend Deborah Thomas was being flown in from Australia, and Lee Tulloch was also attending.

The scale of this launch was unprecedented. Journalists from around the world were flying in first-class to Cannes and then helicoptered into Monte Carlo. We were booked into the magnificent Hôtel de Paris, one of the finest hotels in the world. Lee, Deb and I checked in, pinching ourselves, while the whiny American editors went ballistic when they were informed that the rooms would not be ready for another half an hour. They were 'exhausted' from their Concorde flights. Deborah had come from Sydney and she was ready to run a marathon.

In my experience on press trips, American journalists are incredibly high maintenance. Italians have very lofty standards, but instead of complaining they just show up whenever they like—or not at all—which is maybe preferable to kvetching. The English mainly whinge. I have no opinion on the French because they rarely mingle.

We were then given mock credit cards which we were able to use for anything we required—in the hotel, at the casino, at The Beach Club—and which would then be billed back to Arden. Dinner that evening was at Le Grill on the eighth floor of the Hôtel de Paris, where the roof slid back to reveal a starry night sky, a clever gesture to kick off the lavish PR exercise.

The next day was free (given the Americans needed to recover from the horrendous ordeal of leaving New York). Deborah, Lee and I had the most indulgent day lounging around at the Monte Carlo Beach Club, where hiring a towel is the equivalent of about one week's rent. Thankfully we had our Elizabeth Arden play money. I spent most of the afternoon fixated by the glamorous jetset Euro mothers and their children, wondering why one toddler required two nannies. It became perfectly obvious at sunset, while the mother was slipping out of her Eres bikini, that one nanny is needed to put Junior into his cashmere swimrobe while the other packs up the Chanel tote.

Our hectic schedule included tours of Saint Paul de Vence, long lunches at the world's most famous restaurants and a stroll around the magical medieval village of Eze. But no work as such. We were shown a bottle of the fragrance, saw the advertising images featuring the American actress Daryl Hannah, and told that she would be joining us for a special dinner at the home of Karl Lagerfeld. It was like a dream holiday.

One balmy afternoon, I wandered through the streets surrounding the hotel and came across a store selling vintage postcards. My mother had travelled to Monaco in the late fifties and during her trip sent a card home to her father, a black-and-white vista of Monte Carlo that I had found and placed in an old wooden photo frame. Here, in this poky shop, was exactly the same postcard. I was thrilled. I would post the identical card to my mother, nearly forty years later. I returned to the Hôtel de Paris and rushed excitedly up to the concierge's desk to buy a stamp.

The concierge was chatting to an American man when I interrupted them, but they both turned to me amiably. 'Where did you find this old postcard?' the concierge laughed, and I launched breathlessly into my longwinded family history of the card and what an amazing coincidence it was that I had found it. The American was nodding along, listening politely, asking me good-natured questions and I thought to myself, 'Gosh you're handsome. You look kind of familiar.' We started chatting casually for several minutes and then suddenly it dawned on me. It was Robert Redford.

I must have displayed that creepy star-struck face people get when they realise they are in the presence of a screen idol. His look turned into one that said: 'Damn, she has just clicked who I am.' I then backed clumsily into the old-fashioned telephone cabinet behind me and dialled Deborah's room. 'Get down here,' I hissed. 'Robert Redford is at reception.' Deborah unfortunately had her wet hair up in a towel, and by the time she descended I had turned into a blithering idiot and Mr Redford had beaten a hasty retreat. I did spot him later that afternoon leaving the hotel, and he waved and smiled at me.

I've met many celebrities over the years but that encounter was fun, because it was by chance and the conversation was natural. Until I blew it.

The Sun Moon Stars festivities were still rolling along. At another grand dinner we were presented with a bottle of the fragrance, which was an opaque navy-blue orb etched with, naturally enough, the sun, moon and stars. I'm not sure that it smelt particularly special, but the branding was all very high-end and it felt a bit thirties, which I liked. At the end of dinner the assembled journalists were given a scroll, wrapped with a navy satin ribbon. Upon unfurling the missive we discovered that—officially—each of us had a star named after us. Seriously. There will forever be a star, out there in space, called Kirstie Clements.

By this time Lee, Deb and I had settled into a perpetual clinking of wine glasses, toasting to our ridiculous good fortune. Then the news emerged that Jackie Onassis had passed away. Darryl Hannah was, at the time, dating John F Kennedy Jr, so we were informed that she would be unable to attend at the official dinner. It went ahead regardless, hosted by Karl Lagerfeld at his magnificent villa. It was one of the most memorable evenings in my career. Lagerfeld was at the head table in the centre of the room, surrounded by Princess Caroline and Prince Albert of Monaco, photographer Helmut Newton and his wife Alice Springs, with Michael Hutchence and then girlfriend Helena Christensen. Despite the dinner being very opulent, there was a lovely casualness to the event which meant we could walk back and forth from the terrace (to watch the specially arranged fireworks *naturelment*). I exchanged pleasantries on my way to the bathroom with Prince Albert, and was introduced to Karl for the first time, which thankfully was not to be the last. All of this against the backdrop of a languid May night on the Cote D'Azur with the moonlight shimmering on the surface of the sea.

Once back in Paris I contacted the Arden PR in Australia to thank her for a most remarkable trip and to enquire in which month's issue she would like the story placed. Boy, this was going to have to be a killer piece. She told me she would get back to me, but months went past and there was no word. After a few promptings, the news came through. For reasons unexplained, everything was cancelled. The Sun Moon Stars fragrance wasn't going to launch.

We could forget we'd ever seen it. Unfortunately I no longer have the bottle, which would be a collector's item indeed. But, hey, we all still have our star in the sky.

6

UPHEAVAL

By early 1997 I had very much settled into my life in Paris, and found a happy routine balancing motherhood and work commitments. There were frequent visitors from Australia, and at least twice a year magazine colleagues would arrive for the RTW shows in February and September, which was always a treat. Along with my wonderful friend Charla Carter, there was plenty of good company available, with an expatriate community that included fashion designer Martin Grant, photographer Martyn Thompson, hairdresser David Mallett, journalist Stephen Todd and illustrator James Dignan. But as many Australians who have relocated to cold climates have observed, when your children begin to walk and play, you start to miss our sunny outdoor lifestyle. It's all very well dressing tiny babies up in beige Bonpoint cashmere for the first six months, but when the child is two, and fighting like a Tasmanian Devil as you try to force him into his padded *combinasion*, visions of t-shirts and bare feet at Bronte Beach are never far from your thoughts.

Whenever I was housebound with the twins, I would make a valiant attempt in the afternoons to take them out into the fresh air. Joseph and Sam both detested being dressed. I would begin the Herculean task with the first one, shoving him into his Petit Bateau bodysuit, sweater, overalls, socks, beanie, gloves, boots and ski suit, while he kicked and screamed. The exercise would then be repeated, and by the end I would be pouring a rosé, almost too exhausted to go. We would arrive at the park, with sleeting rain, puddles full of dirt and a subzero wind chill factor, and the gorgeous little things would raise their red-raw faces to me with a look as if to say, 'You think this is fun?'

The miserable weather often meant that I was reduced to taking them to the local McDonalds, so they could at least expend some energy in one of those glass enclosures filled with coloured plastic balls. The big problem was they weren't quite the minimum size or age allowed, so they would become completely submerged and I'd constantly be wading in to fish them out. We went on a summer vacation to Biarritz for two weeks and the sun never came out. Not once. It was too cold to eat ice cream. Joe, Sam and I cried throughout the whole holiday.

One drizzly morning my editor at *Vogue Singapore*, Michal McKay, an incredibly chic woman with a precise ebony bob, rang to share the sad news that the magazine was to close. It was a shame for all, as the team had done a wonderful job, but it also meant that I lost my monthly retainer, which was a serious blow to the household finances.

The news travelled fast and Nancy was on the phone shortly afterwards with a proposition. Would I like to return to Australia to fill the position as her deputy editor? Nancy had already suggested once before that I come back to *Vogue*. A new CEO, Didier Guérin, had recently been appointed, and Nancy confessed that they were not exactly seeing eye to eye. She needed the moral support.

Mourad and I sat down and discussed moving back. I had been asked to return by Condé Nast twice; I believed there wouldn't be a third time. I also truly believed that Sydney would be a better environment to raise young children. In his heart, I don't think Mourad really wanted to come to Australia, as he is very close to his family and was reluctant to leave them. But he agreed to do it for me. I accepted Nancy's offer, agreeing that I would commence in March.

We decided that the twins and I would leave first, and move into my mother's house until we found somewhere to rent. Mourad would follow later, after his car was sold and the apartment packed up. The airfares were booked and purchased, notice given on our lease. I had packed suitcases for the children and myself, and closed my French bank account. With only a few weeks to go before our departure, the apartment phone rang late one night. It was Nancy. She had just been fired.

It was a sickening moment, for both of us. She was understandably upset and the last thing I wanted to say at such an awful time was: 'What's going to happen to me?' Nancy didn't know who had been appointed as her replacement, but she had thoughtfully already clarified with Guérin that my job offer was still in place. I really didn't want the gig anymore, not under these circumstances, but I had no other choice. We couldn't even begin to guess who the new editor would be. 'Okay,' I said to Nancy. 'I'm going to the couture tomorrow. Let me talk to some of the other press and see if I can find out anything.'

After a sleepless night I took the train into the city, and found my seat at the Valentino couture show. A fellow journalist I knew from the *South Sea China Post* was beside me. 'Aren't you going back to *Vogue Australia*?' she said. 'I heard there's a new editor.'

'Yes, I believe so,' I replied, trying to maintain my cool. 'Who is it?'

'Marion Hume, the English journalist,' she said pointing to a woman in a navy-blue pantsuit sitting on the other side of the runway. 'She's over there.'

I already knew Marion, only very slightly, from the circuit. She was a well-respected fashion journalist in London, and had been a recent guest at Australian Fashion Week. Her expert commentary while she was in Sydney must have caught the attention of the powers that be at *Vogue*. No matter, apparently, that she had never run a magazine. After the show had finished, I made my way over and touched her on the arm. 'Ah hello, it's you, Kirstie,' she said in a not unfriendly manner. 'We need to talk.'

Marion was accompanied by her deputy, another British journalist called Alison Veness who had piercing eyes and dark curly hair, and was wearing a full-length greatcoat and staring at me intently. Marion explained that Alison would be moving to Sydney to work with her. 'Come with us, we're going to see Mr Valentino. We can talk in there.' Thus, I found myself perched on a sofa, awkwardly waiting for Valentino in his backstage suite, as his numerous pug dogs pattered around the room. These two Englishwomen would now be in charge of *Vogue Australia*. All I wanted to do was get to the phone to call Nancy.

Guérin had obviously spoken to Marion about my imminent return to Australia, and perhaps because I had been Paris-based and seemed more global, she approved the placement. However, as Alison was now going to fill the role of deputy, and was being relocated to Sydney with both her young daughter and the nanny, I was told I was headed for the beauty department. I had no real problem with that. A job was a job at this point. Within weeks, I had wistfully farewelled Paris and my hospitable in-laws, and was back at my old desk in the *Vogue* office at Greenwich.

I had been away for four years and there had been many other staff changes, not just Nancy's abrupt departure. Karin (now Karin Upton Baker) had been the editor of *Mode* magazine, published by Australian Consolidated Press, since 1995; fashion director Judith Cook had gone, and fashion editor Tory Collison was soon let go by Marion for some inexplicable reason. All the good taste had left the building. There was no denying both Marion and Alison were crack journalists and news-hounds, and I liked both of them personally, but a *Vogue* magazine discipline is completely different to a newspaper one. They spent most of the time in Marion's office with the door closed, hiring UK-based freelancers who wanted to escape a northern hemisphere winter.

It was immensely difficult for the local magazine staff as we were all keen to understand what vision they had for the title. From what I could deduce, the view was particularly British. There was a general belief—also held by the second-rate freelancers who were arriving by the planeload, business-class—that Australians were basically clueless. At a rare planning meeting for the December issue, Marion shared her idea of featuring Kylie Minogue, Nick Cave, Dame Edna Everage and Rolf Harris for God's sake, celebrating at a Christmas party. A number of younger staff looked at me quizzically. They didn't have a clue who Rolf Harris was. Anyway, Rolf would be photographed opening a Christmas cracker, out of which would spill plastic kangaroos. There would be a pavlova. It had nothing to do with producing a *Vogue*; it was more like some comical Royal Command Performance fantasy.

Preferred shooting locations for other fashion stories included Uluru, the desert, Sydney Harbour (so that a water taxi could be included), an AFL stadium complete with players, and a 'typically Aussie' Christmas lunch on Bondi Beach, propped with lounges and torches in the sand. I lost it at that meeting. While various other sycophants were jotting down notes about where to borrow some vintage sofas, I somewhat tetchily raised the point that most of our readers would be at their lovely homes on Christmas Day wearing Gucci sandals and unpacking the Simon Johnson hamper. The only ones who would be on Bondi Beach were British backpackers. It felt like we were producing a magazine for Tourism Australia.

I have never been of the opinion that *Vogue Australia* should continually feature obvious Australian landscapes, although I know many people disagree. Our sun, surf, outdoors lifestyle can be difficult to capture in a very high fashion sense; it requires real artistry to ensure the shoot doesn't end up looking like a mid-range swimwear catalogue. Patrick Russell, who was a star photographer for *Vogue* in the seventies, captured a wonderful sense of Australian sexiness, using handsome male models in Speedos alongside strong, glamorous women to create truly iconic images. Graham Shearer and Richard Bailey, who were both surfers themselves, knew how to project a casual, easy elegance that drew on the incomparable Australian light rather than opting for the obvious and popping the Sydney Opera House in the shot. But most Australian photographers are not in the slightest bit interested in having surf in the background of a shoot, unless you suggest that you were thinking of sending them to the Maldives for eight days. I always felt that the grandeur of the desert can sometimes seem diminished by fashion, and there are now strict Indigenous laws that prevent certain sites, such as Uluru, being shot at all.

I thought our readers didn't necessarily want the focus of the magazine to always be on the local. *Vogue* readers like to dream and be inspired by global references. Australians have always looked outwards; I believe it is one of our greatest strengths. We are also very sensitive if we feel we are being patronised.

Marion experienced a very harsh backlash when she ran an accessories story called 'There's a Huntsman in My Handbag' in 1997, which was a creepy set of improbable scenarios, incorporating spiders, snakes and other various dangerous antipodean creatures, and featuring the actress Rachel Griffiths. I actually thought it was quite funny but the readers were aghast, and the tone was interpreted as condescending. There were fashion shoots featuring barbeques and a great deal of the styling made use of the rubber thong, often worn with a couture dress. The idea was probably that it projected a cool insouciance, but to me it just looked sloppy.

I think Marion respected my opinion, and she did listen to my concerns sometimes. I could see it was difficult for her. Both she and Alison worked around the clock. Marion seemingly had been told nothing about budgets, so costs were going through the roof, and she was surrounded by quite a few toadies who were more interested in advancing their personal careers. Nobody would question her decisions, even if they privately thought she was wrong. Many times I thought people were taking advantage of her.

There was a particularly disastrous moment when it was decided to fly in a top US photographer to shoot several stories for a big issue. Business-class tickets were booked and a five-star hotel was arranged, not only for him but also for his assistants and his preferred hairdresser and makeup artist. If someone had mentioned it to me beforehand, I would have rung the alarm bells. Why fly in an entire team? It's far more controllable to sprinkle in some staffers and local freelancers that you already know and trust, otherwise a cliquey international crew will generally ignore your brief and do anything they want, while you sign the cheques and fret over the mini bar charges.

As it transpired, the photographer had clearly regretted his decision to come to Sydney en route over the Pacific. When he arrived he made limited contact with the editorial team, shot one quick fashion story, and was then asked if he would like to see locations for the next stories that had been planned. He demanded a limousine, and spent a day being driven to various scenic destinations in and around greater Sydney. It was debatable if he in fact saw anything at all because he never removed his dark sunglasses, but upon his return to the hotel he declared there wasn't any location in Australia worth shooting, and he and his team flew home, leaving charges that the CFO never fully recovered from. It was a debacle, and I felt badly for Marion.

Sales were plummeting, management was circling and the international advertisers were leaving in droves. I could feel the downhill spiral. Marion put a great deal of focus on the local Australian designers, who loved all the attention at the beginning until she dared to criticise some of them in print. What, a Brit telling us we're not good enough? The press, who were fawning when she arrived, then turned on her.

Designers also stuck the knife in, stating—probably disingenuously—they had been 'thinking' of advertising in the magazine but now they wouldn't. Marion was used to being an outspoken critic; she was accomplished and she was fair. It was what her reputation was built on. But it's a newspaper mentality. In magazines we criticise by omission.

If we considered that you weren't good enough to be in *Vogue*, then you simply weren't in *Vogue*. An editor-in-chief whose main mission is to create a luxury environment is not expected to point out anything substandard or ordinary. Like Pollyanna, we concentrate only on the wonderful. And don't even think about writing or saying anything remotely negative about an advertiser. Even a potential one. It's a minefield that's best managed with your mouth shut.

One fraught afternoon, when *Vogue*'s last watch client had just cancelled their forward ad bookings because their editorial in the latest issue was so ugly, my phone rang. It was Karin Upton Baker. *Mode* magazine was about to morph into *Harper's Bazaar and Mode* (the word *Mode* would drop off after a few months) and Karin was putting together a new team for the launch. Would I like to be the associate editor? I didn't even go in for an interview, or ask about the salary. The conversation was, 'Yes please! Yay! When can I start, shall I tell management now, can I, can I?!'

I'm not a very savvy negotiator when it comes to my own salary. My motivation has always been the job itself, and the people I would be working alongside; never, ever the money. The nine months I had spent back at *Vogue* had been fraught and disorganised, and I was thrilled to be going to *Bazaar*. I had always liked working with Karin, and my great friend Eric Matthews, who had moved from *Vogue Australia* to take up the art directorship of *Vogue Singapore*, was now the new art director of *Bazaar*. I knew Karin would be a first-rate editor-in-chief, and that we could, especially given *Vogue*'s current state, make *Bazaar* a success. It was a dream offer, and very timely. It is always preferable not to go down with a sinking ship.

When you resign from a magazine to go to a rival company you are sometimes instructed to leave immediately, depending on your position and how many company secrets you possess. It's all very dramatic in fashion. I once saw an advertising rep get frogmarched to the lift, and as the doors were slowly closing, her manager threw a pot plant at her. I didn't exactly have the company EBIT statement at my fingertips, so my departure was relatively cordial, although I did leave the same day that I handed in my notice. One of the fashion editors strolled into my office as I was packing up my desk and I thought, how sweet, she's come to say goodbye and wish me well. But no. She asked me if she could have the keys to the beauty cupboard, where all the free products were kept. It really had turned into *Lord of the Flies* and I was relieved to be leaving the island.

Karin and the team had finished their first issue of *Harper's Bazaar and Mode* by the time I arrived in late 1997, and were in the midst of organising the launch party. Nicole Kidman was on the cover, dressed in Dior couture, art directed by Eric in London and styled by Charla Carter, who had joined as a contributor. Tory Collison would soon come on board as fashion editor. Everything felt right again.

Karin has great personal style, and was famously fastidious about details, so the gala launch on the ground floor of Sydney's Customs House was a supremely elegant affair. At the end of Karin's speech thousands of miniature paper covers of the launch issue fluttered down from above, and in a lovely Surrealist touch, with a gesture to the heritage of the masthead, guests were handed the issue by gloved arms protruding from a large white box. The crowd, consisting mostly of advertisers that were pulling out of *Vogue*, were clearly delighted to now have a classy alternative option.

The months I spent at *Vogue* working under Marion, and the time I would spend at *Harper's Bazaar* under Karin were, in retrospect, when I learned some of my most valuable lessons in publishing. My greatest understanding, in respect to what was happening at *Vogue*, came mainly from observing what not to do. Working for brands as esteemed as *Vogue* and *Bazaar* highlighted how crucial it is to maintain a standard: a consistency and an integrity of purpose that flows through every element of the business, from the stationery to the sales presentation to the crucial September issue. There has to be a long-term vision that is shared and understood by every staff member, rather than 'this will do for now', 'this will be great for me personally', or a quick sell-out to make budget. As is true for any business, it can only be achieved by employing the right people. Luxury brands are precarious, and while everyone likes to think they know exactly how to run one, very few people do.

While super-brands like *Vogue* may appear to be unassailable, I had witnessed first-hand that they are not. They also act as an irresistible magnet to frauds, wankers and wannabes.

The *Bazaar* editorial team was talented, as was the sales department, led by commercial dynamo Lynette Phillips. Everyone was on the same mission, and the magazine made an immediate impact on launch. The managing editor, Louise Upton, didn't like me very much for some reason, but she was very good at her job and I knew how to do mine, so we coexisted. I'm not of the belief that everybody has to love you, and socialise with you after work. As long as you treat everyone with respect, and vice versa, then I think office politics are something to avoid wherever possible. Of course I can bitch along with the best of them—part of that is just office camaraderie—but you know when a line gets crossed and it becomes pure nastiness. I worked with some snakes later in my career, and in my experience they never last. Eventually—although it does take longer than you would hope, and while they may topple some good people on the way through—the torch will shine on them and they will be exposed. Whereas those who concentrate on the task at hand and on doing their best work will always have a career.

In one of the early *Harper's Bazaar* issues we decided to feature modelling great Lauren Hutton, who was in Australia for David Jones. Tory was styling and I was to interview Ms Hutton. I was absolutely thrilled at the prospect of meeting her, as she is one of the true trailblazers of the industry and from what I'd read, a real feminist ballbreaker. She was, but unfortunately it was my balls she was going to break.

She disliked me intensely on sight, but then it seemed she didn't like any of the women on the job. She refused to let the makeup artist do her makeup and snapped at everyone except for the male photographer. By the end of what was a long day she turned on me and said she was far too tired to do the interview, which was more than fine with me because I had lost all interest in talking to her.

We did end up putting her on the cover, thinking that featuring a beautiful, mature woman would make a powerful statement, but sales were terrible. It is a truism in the magazine business that what women say they want to see on a cover, they don't always follow through and buy. Mature, plus-size, un-retouched or different ethnicities, they are all, to this day—unfortunately—a gamble. The safest sales still come from a young, slim, pretty, non-threatening blonde or light brunette with not too much makeup or hair product.

A better experience was a shoot with another supermodel, the inimitable Jerry Hall, who had been brought to Australia by designer Charlie Brown. She was going through her divorce with Mick Jagger at the time and was clearly preoccupied, but she was a sweetheart to the whole awestruck team. I met her again many years later with her daughter Georgia May Jagger, in 2010, when we judged Fashions on the Field together at the races in Melbourne. She had the same easy, friendly manner and was just as stunning. I didn't mention it to her on either occasion, but when, at age fourteen, I saw Hall in the Bryan Ferry video for 'Let's Stick Together', I cried myself to sleep because I realised I would never be as glamorous as her. (I also thought the same thing about Debbie Harry in fishnets performing 'In the Flesh'.) Clearly I got over it, but Jerry Hall is certainly one-of-a-kind, old-school fabulous.

* * *

Things had gone from bad to worse over at *Vogue*, and in late 1998 Marion was out. The press had been giving her a relentless beating prior to her sacking, but conveniently forgot all that when she was fired and began righteously speculating on the reason she was dismissed, suggesting it was because of her forthright opinions on Australian designers and the fact that she had put a 'black girl'—Naomi Campbell—on her first cover. A fictional moral and intellectual showdown between Marion and the suits was now invented, by the same hypocrites who had previously ripped her to shreds. The point was entirely missed that her departure was about declining profit and circulation. Marion was replaced by another Englishwoman, Juliet Ashworth, who had been recruited from tabloid magazines.

It appeared management had decided that in order to stop the free-fall, *Vogue* should cast off some of its elitist notions and move into the area of middle and mass market. Do it all in fact, so it could cover every area: luxury *and* mid-market and mass. Think how lucrative that would that be! It's a theory I would hear over and over again from various newcomers (and, my special favourite, their wives who don't in fact read the magazine or own a nice handbag) during my career at *Vogue*, and it's a giant mistake. It's a dangerous move to drastically redraw the borders of an iconic luxury brand.

Harper's Bazaar was steadily gaining traction in the minds of both consumers and advertisers. The previous year, as editor of *Mode*, Karin and the publisher Patricia Connolly had established an invitation-only hospitality space at the Sydney Showgrounds during Australian Fashion Week in 1997, and it became the place to be, serving champagne and chicken sandwiches to the buzzy fashion crowd all day and into the evening. Apparently, Karin's standards were so exacting she had the chicken sandwiches tasted four times before she approved them, which I loved. Even though I was with *Vogue* then, Karin knew it was through circumstances beyond my control given Nancy's abrupt removal, and was gracious enough to let me station myself there between fashion shows. By May 1998 it had turned into 'Bar *Bazaar*' and it was an early masterstroke of branding. It was standing room only most of the time, providing a chic retreat where everyone in fashion and society could gossip, be interviewed, be filmed or be seen. *Harper's Bazaar Australia* was on the map, and I was very content to be one of the team.

Owned by the Hearst Corporation in the US, and published as a joint venture by Australian Consolidated Press, *Bazaar*'s impressive performance had obviously registered with its international management. In April 1999 the influential and much-admired editor-in-chief of American *Harper's Bazaar*, Liz Tilberis, sadly passed away after a battle with ovarian cancer. Karin was invited to take the editor's chair in

New York for an unspecified period until a replacement was found. She was also a contender for the permanent role. It was an incredible honour for an editor from Australia, and we were all thrilled for her.

Louise and I held the fort and Karin would call in each afternoon to check on things and supply us with the most delicious gossip from the US *Bazaar* offices. Australian Fashion Week rolled around and, as Karin was still away, I became the unofficial host of Bar *Bazaar*. During a quiet period, when the blowdryers were off and the manicure stations empty, I was standing at the bar eating yet another chicken sandwich when Robyn Holt walked in.

I had known Robyn for many years, and admired her enormously. We first met at *Vogue* when I was on reception—she and I always laugh when I remind her that she was pregnant with her daughter Hannah at the time but I never realised, because everything was hidden under the layers of her uber on-trend Katie Pye dresses.

Robyn had been the beauty editor of *Vogue*, the editor of *Vogue Living* and for the past few years, the managing director of Yves Saint Laurent Beauté. Chic, funny and smart, she was also one of Nancy's best friends. I offered her a glass of champagne and as we were chatting she said quietly: 'How would you like to be the editor of *Vogue*?'

I'm not entirely sure, but I probably spluttered in amazement. Robyn then confessed that she had just accepted the role as managing director of Condé Nast. I was to keep it confidential but she felt I was the right person to replace Juliet. She asked me to prepare a document outlining my vision and what I thought I could bring to the magazine, and we agreed to meet again in a few days to discuss the role.

Not once, in what had been my fourteen years in publishing, had I considered editing *Vogue*. I had never thought about what came next or coveted someone else's job. I had no desire in particular to be on top. I loved what I did, and was always happy in the positions that I had held. Certainly, throughout the years, I have witnessed a number of people enter the business with teeth-gnashing career ambition, but that type of person unnerves me. I have generally found that the very ambitious make terrible decisions, because everything is about them. When Robyn offered me the role I did not in all honesty think: 'Yes, yes, at last, finally the job I deserve, editor of *Vogue*!' I was not interested in the status; I never have been. I just liked making magazines.

I went home and thought, 'I think I could do it. I've worked in every part of the business. I know good staff when I see them.' From my long experience I knew that making *Vogue* a success was, ultimately, not going to be about me and how marvellous and clever I was. It would depend entirely on the team we put together. From reception upwards.

There was more good news. In a wonderfully ironic twist, Nancy Pilcher was going back to *Vogue* in a senior editorial position that covered Condé Nast's interests in both Australia and Asia Pacific. She was going to be installed in Guérin's now vacated office. The former workspace of the same man who had unceremoniously fired her two years before. Nancy moved in and promptly painted the wall behind her an Hermès shade of orange. The colour of intelligence.

Rumours were flying around the marketplace that Ashworth was about to be replaced, and the most persistent conjecture was that the editorship of *Vogue* would be given to Karin. No one suspected that I had the gig, and it was agonising trying to keep it secret. I can't be sure, but I think someone at ACP began to have their suspicions.

Karin was due back from New York imminently, and I suddenly received an out of the blue offer from *Harper's Bazaar* management.

The idea was that I would become editor of *Bazaar*, as Karin was going to be promoted to editorial director of both *Bazaar* and *Belle* magazines.

I was feeling slightly overwhelmed at this point with two offers on the table, but in my heart I was committed to *Vogue*. I needed to stall. I didn't want to accept the position at *Bazaar* and then go back on my word. Yet if I declined, they would sense something was up. It was a matter of mere days before Juliet was to be informed her services were no longer required at *Vogue*. As soon as that happened, Robyn was going to ring me in the *Bazaar* office and I would then immediately hand in my notice. I disliked feeling so underhanded, but legally this is how things have to play out. I had not planned or executed any ideas that I intended to take to *Vogue*, or approached any staff. It was an honour to be offered the editorship of *Bazaar* and I was grateful for my time there, but the idea of rebuilding *Vogue* was too enticing.

It was amazing to me that with no real preconceived notion of where I was heading, I should be offered the editorship of Australia's top two luxury titles simultaneously. But I would never have considered returning to *Vogue* if I did not believe in the new management. The best masthead in the world means nothing without the right people in charge. I believed in the power of *Vogue*. But I also knew things were not handed to you on a platter. When you edit *Vogue*, you are under a microscope. You had to be smarter and faster than the competition, and I wanted to accept that challenge.

7

FASHION FIXATIONS

Looking back at my performance in sewing classes at Sylvania Heights Primary School, it seems ludicrous that I would end up working in the fashion industry. I'm surprised I wasn't put off fashion for life by my teacher Mrs Smith. A spiteful, dour woman who always had pins between her pursed lips, Mrs Smith delighted in skewering those students who weren't quite up to par with their needlework.

One afternoon, as I was hunched over a stupid pinwheel trying to embroider a chain stitch, she turned on me and demanded I do it all over again because it wasn't straight. I made the mistake of admitting that I hated the whole exercise and I didn't envisage a future that included embroidery anyway. This made her so angry she kept the whole class back after the bell rang until I completed the task. All the girls were hissing 'C'mon Clements' and throwing things at me, as my tears plopped down on the pinwheel and Mrs Smith stood over me with a malevolent grin. I distinctly remember having a Scarlett O'Hara 'as God is my witness I will never pick up a sewing needle again' moment, and went straight home to tell my mother about my humiliation. My dear mum immediately wrote a letter to the school, reminding them of my academic prowess (Year Four spelling bee champion) and demanded that I be excused from sewing classes. I also made her put in a paragraph stating that a girls-only sewing class was sexist. It may have been the headmaster's little joke, but as a result I was sent to canework lessons with the boys. That too was tedious, irrelevant and possibly cancerous, because the tough guys in the class were constantly setting fire to whatever useless knick-knack they made, but I stayed just to prove a point. Eventually the teachers allowed me to go to the library, where I read and wrote ghost stories instead.

As luck would have it, sewing was compulsory in my first year at Sylvania High School. There was just something about sewing machines and me. It was as if I attracted a poltergeist every time I went near one. By the time I had clumsily threaded the needle and then jammed and unjammed the bloody thing ten or so times, the rest of the class would have run up a wraparound maxi skirt while my fabric would be in shreds. My high school teacher eventually took pity on me and just let me watch the other girls. To this day I have never so much as sewn on a button and I never will.

Being a teenage girl in the Sutherland Shire in the seventies is something we could all later relate to through Kathy Lette and Gabrielle Carey's seminal novel *Puberty Blues*, published in 1979. Sylvania High School was ground zero for the stultifying surfie culture the book brings to life. I started there in 1974, and while Lette and Carey were several years ahead of me, I recall they were always a little eccentric.

There was one occasion when they both arrived at morning assembly wearing black glasses and carrying walking canes, pretending to be blind. I thought they were oddly amusing, but it was best to hide any individual or intelligent thoughts if you were to fit in with the dominant behaviours that prevailed.

There was a very strict dress code that none of us dared to stray from, mostly revolving around high-waisted shorts with front pleats in Hawaiian-print cotton. I had to pay friends who could sew to make some for me. The shorts were accessorised with 'slaps' (velvet thongs with a rattan base that smelt like a wet dog after one wear), clunkies (a wooden platform wedge sandal), or—the height of Cronulla chic—a platform Dr Scholl's sandal. I desperately wanted a pair of Scholl's, but my mother, who owned an upmarket children's clothing boutique in the Cronulla high street called Minnie's Inn Shop, refused to buy me any. She had noticed all the surfie chicks shuffling down the street in them, and had apparently been revolted by their dry cracked heels.

My girlfriends and I also shopped in the hippy stores, for long Indian-print wraparound skirts (perfect with aforementioned clunkies), stacks of thin, multicoloured and patterned plastic bracelets, and strawberry musk oil. Jeans were flared and high waisted, put back with boob tubes or a satin handkerchief top. Bikinis were crochet. Eye shadow was bright sky-blue, bought from Grace Bros at Miranda Fair.

When I think back, Miranda Fair shopping mall perhaps shaped my future more than I could ever have predicted. There was a newsagency at the front of the centre that imported a UK magazine for teenage girls called *Pink*. I was obsessed with it. *Pink* covered fashion, beauty, pop bands, the tone was clever and fun, and I was completely addicted. Whoever edited it was a genius. The newsagency only ordered one or two copies, so every Saturday morning I would walk the three kilometres to the mall and sit outside by myself, often in the cold, waiting for it to open so I wouldn't miss out. I was disconsolate that Australia didn't have a Boots chemist so I could buy lipstick for 29p. That I ended up being the beauty editor of *Vogue* now makes such perfect sense.

By the age of fifteen, my girlfriends and I had started going to local pubs and discos, dressed to kill (and get past the doorman) in harem pants, lip gloss, stiletto mules and clutch bags. But I hated the music. I had always liked glam rock: the first single I ever bought was 'Jeepster' by T Rex, I'd seen Bryan Ferry and Gary Glitter at the Hordern Pavilion, I was a member of the David Bowie fan club and I made my own Bowie scrapbooks. The longer I lived in the Shire, the less I fitted in. I couldn't stand the beach culture, and all the abuse that would be hurled at you when you walked past a gang of surfies. Everyone was stoned and 'bonging on' all the time, listening to The Doobie Brothers or the Eagles. No garden hose was safe. Nobody wanted to go to university, travel or even read. The mere sound of rugby league commentary on the radio on Sunday afternoons depressed me and reminded me how out of place I was. The only people who looked potentially interesting to me were the bikies, because I appreciated their outfits, but they were a little too scary.

In 1978 I began working at a shoe store in Sylvania Heights for a few afternoons a week after school and on Saturday mornings. It was also a ballet supply store. I absolutely loved that job; unpacking all the new shoes when they came in, and just being surrounded by the gorgeous pale-pink satin-pointe slippers and headbands.

The owner's daughter, Leonie, was a year or so older than me, and had a boyfriend with a car and great taste in music. One morning, when we were both working together in the store, she told me that she and her boyfriend were going into the city to see a band. Would I like to come? Saturday night, I was sixteen years old and we were headed for the Grand Hotel on George Street, opposite Central Station in the heart of Sydney.

The front of the bar was your average rough Aussie pub, with a ragtag bunch of drinkers of all ages. You had to walk through to the back and down a few steps to a windowless room that had another small bar. This is where the bands played. No one checked ID. I walked into the gloom nervously and looked around. It was full of punks with safety pins in their noses and ears, studded leather jackets and skinny black jeans. There were hardly any girls, and the ones that were there looked formidable. The support band started, a sort of punkish/rockabilly outfit called Tommy and The Dipsticks. Then came the more hardcore punk band: Johnny Dole and the Scabs. The crowd was drinking and spitting and pogoing. It was the most exciting thing I had ever seen. The music, the energy, the clothes. I had discovered like-minded people from all backgrounds; people who loved music, film and fashion. That night changed my life.

In a wonderful stroke of luck, my lovely Aunt Fay and her husband Tony lived in a vast terrace house in Bondi Junction. After my epiphany at The Grand, I became obsessed with the punk scene. I could stay at my aunt's, which was central to all the venues, and she didn't care what time I came home. She would also let my best friends from school, Robyn and Jenny, stay. That was the end of the horrible disco clothes and the Shire.

Our new uniform consisted of black or blue jeans that we had to get run in by Jenny (who could manage a sewing machine) to make them into super-skinny stovepipes. We wore black sneakers, t-shirts and khaki army disposal jackets with red lipstick, black nail polish and loads of eyeliner. We made friends with a lot of the guys in the bands, who were really very sweet when they weren't spitting and pogoing. We followed bands like the Urban Guerillas, X, Radio Birdman, The Boys Next Door and The Saints. All the pubs had live music, and no one cared if you were underage. There were never any problems. We were there for the music and the fashion, not to glass each other.

Once I fell into the band scene there was no going back to the Shire. My mother knew I had a thirst for adventure, and she trusted me. Mum had travelled a great deal as a young woman, taking the ship to London and having numerous European adventures before she met my father Joseph. She always encouraged me to follow my instincts. So a few months later I had the clerical job at a stockbroker's office in Clarence Street, and had moved into my first apartment in Kings Cross, which I shared with a girlfriend. I had escaped from the stifling conformity of the suburbs! Now the fashion experimentation really kicked in.

Everybody on the punk music scene had no money to speak of, as they were all in bands and on the dole. Over the next few years I would live in shared accommodation in many dubious terrace houses and apartments around Darlinghurst, Kings Cross and Surry Hills, listening to Iggy Pop and the Buzzcocks while various aspiring bass players practised the opening riff to 'Public Image' in the lounge room. The girls, rather than the boys, tended to have jobs, as for some of us it was important to have milk, tea and toilet paper in the house. Because we were all broke, clothes were trawled from disposal stores, op shops and markets, and customised to suit. Everyone looked amazing. We became terrible image snobs. I suppose in some way I had merely swapped the uniform of the suburbs for another tribal code—but this one was far more cool.

The boys were all super skinny because they lived on cigarettes and flagons of wine, and only ate the day their dole cheques came in. They all had whippet-thin black suits, with dyed black hair *à la* Bob Dylan in his heroin period, or were bleached blonde in leather jackets like Paul Simonon from The Clash. We had very specific groups we would cross over with: rockabillies, punks, mods, New Romantics and weird, arty New Zealanders in vintage clothes, yes; hippies, pub rock bogans and surfies—good God no.

My girlfriends and I adopted another look that was based around black mini skirts, fishnet stockings, ripped sweatshirts, hoop earrings and bleached blonde hair, later dyed bright pink with Crazy Colour. On one trip back to the Shire to visit Mum she refused to walk through the local shopping centre with me. I think I was also wearing white, short gumboots with matte black tights—probably not my sartorial zenith. Then a boy I was mad about told me I looked like a fifties B-grade movie star. I was thrilled with this (now I come to think of it) somewhat backhanded compliment. My new fashion predilection was for full fifties skirts, angora sweaters, stiletto heels and diamante drop earrings. The op shops were a treasure trove, because at that time they were full of fifties and sixties originals that didn't cost the earth. My fashion icon was Ava Gardner, and the mother, Nancy Kelly, from the 1956 horror thriller movie *The Bad Seed*. The forties and the fifties have always been my preferred style decades, and in later years I would shop at Prada to achieve a similar effect.

Makeup was of course crucial to our sense of theatrics. The punk era required us to be porcelain pale, so that was the end of sunlight for me. I retreated indoors at the age of sixteen and never tanned again. My friend Gabriel Wilder and I used to save up to buy Shiseido foundation No. 1, the lightest and most matte base on the market. We wore thick brush strokes of black liquid eyeliner, false lashes, bright-red lipstick and hot-pink blush. The general effect was probably something near Kabuki makeup, and five shades off the right colour for our natural complexions, but it's a look I love and have never quite gotten over. I've toned it down a bit now as is appropriate for my age, but I fully intend taking it back up again when I'm seventy, along with blood-red nails and men's silk lounging pyjamas.

Our fashion sense was also strongly influenced by many of the international bands that were touring; the scene was so small and we normally met them somehow. Siouxsie and The Banshees, The Cure, Simple Minds, The Pretenders, The Stranglers, Lou Reed, Nico and Elvis Costello all came into our social orbit and so we seesawed between Goth (all black), New Romantic (pirate shirts and high-waisted black pants) and Buffalo Girl (brown leather distressed men's jackets with long full cotton skirts). At Paddington Markets one Saturday morning in 1982, Gabriel and I spotted the real Paul Simonon, bass player of The Clash, buying a fifties lamp. We bowled up and nervously introduced ourselves to him, and he very generously put our names on the door list for every one of The Clash's Sydney concerts at the Capitol.

Music informed everything I chose to wear as did, increasingly, cinema. If we weren't seeing bands, we were at the movies, great old theatres like the Mandarin and the Valhalla in Glebe, getting an education in seminal film. Every house had a Valhalla cinema schedule poster stuck on the back of the toilet door; it was like ubiquitous wallpaper. It was around about this period I decided that if ever in doubt, dress like Anouk Aimee in *La Dolce Vita*. Or Grace Kelly in *Rear Window*.

I made two extended trips to Europe in the early eighties and my fashion recollections are reflective of the trends at the time—black jeans, a black overcoat, Cuban-heeled boots and a PLO scarf was something of a uniform in London. Another extended stay in Greece involved cheesecloth goddess dresses, gold chain belts and—I shudder to admit—I may have even tied one of those gold leather plaits around my forehead, but that was a momentary aberration. On a trip to Italy in 1984 I finally cemented what is pretty much my style up until today.

I was travelling through Rome with my friends Bernard and Michael. Bernard was a huge fan of Italian culture. We had been to all the Italian film festivals together back in Sydney. One afternoon, we walked into the Fiorucci store and I spotted a cream overcoat. It was a perfect fifties duster coat, with printed lining. Add black cropped cigarette pants, ballet flats and cat-eye glasses and that was it. I don't stray far from this style right up until today. Fiorucci was quite trendy then, and not inexpensive. Considering I had shopped vintage all my life, this was the first real 'label' I had ever bought. I had that coat for years; it never dated. Bernard bought one very similar. He wore it with loafers and no socks, with his black hair in a quiff, and in doing so managed to look like Marcello Mastroianni.

It was liberating to spend the early part of my youth playing with clothes and finding my own style, without the tyranny of being influenced by expensive labels. I feel sad when I hear young girls today—especially teenagers—saying, 'I love Givenchy and Balenciaga', and you know it's unlikely they have ever read a book about the original designer. I think an eighteen-year-old with a luxury designer bag has missed out on a lot, not the least the excitement of it taking fifteen years to save up and buy one for yourself.

It was this fifties-Fellini vibe I was channelling when I started at *Vogue*. Judith Cook appreciated what I was trying to achieve on my very limited budget (my salary on the reception desk was $81 per week). She still reminds me that I used to wear ballet slippers and headbands and red lipstick. All the editors at *Vogue* understood that style is not a slavish devotion to labels. When you work in fashion, it stands to reason that you are going to follow trends, but where it goes wrong is if the trend doesn't suit you personally.

When I moved to Paris in 1994, I moved into what I now think of my post-war Paris period. I had it all: the red lips, my hair up in combs in a Victory Roll. I wore silk crepe, forties floral-print dresses by Cacharel, with Robert Clergerie forties-style black suede sandals and black fishnet stockings. My perfume was Shalimar by Guerlain or Chanel No. 5, as they were redolent of the period. One afternoon, I noticed a good-looking young man had been following me for blocks. He finally approached me at the traffic lights and said timidly: 'I've been walking behind you for a long time. You are like a woman from another era, the smell of your fragrance, the way you are dressed, your stockings, the sound that your heels make on the cobblestones.' I was thrilled he understood my intention. He then asked if I would have a glass of champagne with him. I did, of course. It's heartening when someone appreciates that you put some thought into how you look.

8

THE EDITOR'S CHAIR

I began at *Vogue* as the receptionist just as the September 1985 issue was on stand. Now here I was starting as editor, with the September 1999 issue just about to launch.

September issues are traditionally the biggest during the calendar year because they contain the most advertising and editorial pages. This one also happened to be *Vogue Australia*'s fortieth anniversary issue, and two parties and exhibitions had been planned for both Sydney and Melbourne. I literally walked into events I had made no contribution to whatsoever, which felt terribly awkward. All I wanted to do was get to my desk and fix the magazine. The way it looked, there was nothing to celebrate. Circulation had taken a massive drop and there were no forward ad bookings. There was one page for the October issue, but it was FOC (free of charge) to compensate for a mistake made with the client in the previous edition. At least Robyn Holt had a sense of humour about the state of affairs. We spent a few minutes in her office grimly amusing ourselves by moving the single ad around the empty magazine grid, seeing where it looked best.

I had no time to start the November issue from scratch, so I kept and cleaned up what had already been commissioned, submitted and was passable. The rest of the magazine I filled with lifts. 'Lifts' are stories that have already appeared in other Condé Nast magazines that are usually available for free, or at a much less expensive rate than it would cost to produce yourself. Financial controllers are big fans of lifts, for obvious reasons. Readers hate them; a savvy reader also buys international magazines, so there can be an overlap in what they are being presented.

There was also—rightly so—an element of reader indignation about us not using enough homegrown talent, and we were sometimes accused, unfairly, of lacking our own ideas. Lifts have become almost obligatory for most licensed titles now, as editors are no longer allocated editorial budgets that can cover the costs of creating every page from scratch. *Vogue*s that are owned and operated by Condé Nast tend to produce all their own material, whereas titles that are under licence to proprietors in other regions, such as Australia, are generally a mix of original material and lifts. I believe there is a place for well-chosen lifts in a luxury title, to make sure all the talent represented consistently remains first-rate. It was not always possible for us to secure the top international models or celebrities of the moment, which is why we sometimes needed to rely on republishing fashion stories and articles from our sister publications such as US, British or Paris *Vogue*. But now the cost pressure in the magazine industry to repurpose non-original material is enormous. The day is fast approaching when a magazine and its website will only be full of lifts, promotional shots handed out by clients, and staff Instagrams. And there will be a whole tier of upper management scratching their heads, wondering why circulation is tumbling and blaming the editor.

It would never occur to them that the reader had been shortchanged.

* * *

The first steps in setting *Vogue* on the right course was to appoint a crack team, which in turn meant letting go of some of the incumbent staff and contributors. I will be eternally grateful to the then editorial business manager Georgette Johnson, and Nancy, who both helped me through the awful process that is terminating someone's employment. While never pleasant, there is an added level of emotion that surrounds working for *Vogue*. It has been successfully positioned over the years as so elite, and so special, that staff can lose their own identity and become overly attached to the brand.

It is a perception that is both positive and negative. On one hand, *Vogue* attracts people who are the best in their field, and who see the opportunity to work for *Vogue* as the pinnacle of their careers. It meant that you could hire the best and, sadly for them, pay the least.

On the other hand, it is intensely alluring to poseurs, social climbers and those on a quest for personal glory. I would say one of my essential tasks as editor—right until the bitter end—was to spot the frauds. *Vogue* could open doors and offer remarkable opportunities to its staff and contributors, so it was vitally important to establish a culture that meant no one could abuse the system and take advantage. We needed to be exemplary in our behaviour, and have manners and standards higher than others in the industry. In 1999 we were going to have to build the brand, and its integrity, back from scratch. If you want to represent *Vogue*, and bask in the cachet that comes with it, you better make sure you can walk the talk.

My first hiring was to poach fashion editor Tory Collison back from *Bazaar*, and she immediately got to work on the main story and cover for the December issue, shooting with Richard Bailey and featuring top Australian model Alyssa Sutherland.

I then began recruiting a new editorial team, starting with the fashion editor from *Marie Claire*, Gabriele Mihajlovksi. I have huge respect for *Marie Claire*'s long-time editor Jackie Frank, and she is clearly wonderful at training staff; I would also steal Naomi Smith back from her a few years later.

One of the best decisions I ever made was to retain the services of Leigh Ann Pow, who was already at *Vogue* as an editorial features assistant. With a background in newspapers, street magazines and the editorship of *Smash Hits* under her belt, Leigh Ann was everything you needed to be in magazines: hardworking, adaptable, honest, smart, a stickler for details and a team player. She also possessed a faultless bullshit detector. Leigh Ann went on to hold various editorial positions, eventually becoming associate editor. She was the most loyal of colleagues for my entire editorship.

The next important appointment was art director, a role that is clearly crucial to a magazine. My inherited art director was a young Spaniard called Simone and while he seemed lovely and was no doubt talented, there was one small problem; he didn't speak any English. Apparently my predecessor had no issue with that, but I thought sign language and Spanish/English dictionaries were likely to hold up proceedings somewhat and as we really needed to get cracking on the redesign of the January 2000 issue, so I set about looking for a replacement.

An accomplished art director is an editor's best ally. The creative design of a magazine is the most important, and yet most nebulous element, because it is conceptual. As an editor you can easily recognise bad writing when you read it. The same goes for fashion styling—the mistakes are immediately apparent. But with art direction the evaluation becomes more complex. You know bad design when you see it. You may know what would improve it. But it can be difficult to articulate or even imagine what would make it great. That particular artistic process is intangible and limitless. Unless you suddenly turned into Fabien Baron overnight, you have to trust the instincts and abilities of your art department. There's nothing that will cause an art director to shut up shop faster than if you walk up behind them, stare at their computer screen and opine: 'You know, I think the type would look better in blue.'

Editors can develop a God complex and believe they are the authority on everything, but it was not a position I ever assumed. I had learned certain truisms during my time in publishing, and I had an overall vision for the magazine, but I was also well aware there were people who were superior to me in other areas. The most pressing concern was to restore excellence and polish in every area, but there is no blueprint for that. There were key words we would follow that would guide our philosophy, such as beautiful, intelligent, first-rate. This approach stayed firm throughout my years as editor, but the execution of it would change constantly.

Some of my ideas were a quick win, such as improving the fashion pages and the covers by hiring more appropriate stylists and photographers. Other initiatives were more trial and error, in terms of type and layout. I knew I would make some mistakes. Collaboration was essential. My mantra is to surround yourself with people who are great at what they do, have an informed opinion, and are willing to push back on you when they think it's necessary. I don't believe in micromanaging, and I have never seen people thrive under it, especially creatives. Staff need perimeters but not edicts. We were constantly seeking to improve every area, whether it was a tweaking of the headings and introductions, a new 'run of book' (the order in which the pages and sections run), a new columnist or a complete redesign. No issue is ever perfect; there is no foolproof formula. But if you think that the magazine is the best it could ever be, you should probably think about leaving.

As the new managing director of Condé Nast, Robyn Holt was a firm believer in the power of harnessing and encouraging the staff's intellectual and emotional intelligence. That she was a savvy business person was a given, but her ability to make every one of us feel that we were on an important and ultimately successful path together was remarkable. Behind a closed door in her office, I would be aghast over the just-released readership figures and she would be tearing her hair out over numerous financial challenges, frantically chewing a Nicorette—but we never let the troops see that.

One of her first steps was to have the offices evaluated for feng shui, and we took the recommended steps afterwards in the hope of achieving a more positive flow of energy. Whether anyone actually believed in it or not, the exercise went down extremely well with the staff as a gesture, and resulted in a logical redesign of the space that would allow different departments to communicate more freely with one another. She walked the floor every day, commenting and enthusing on whatever the editorial staff were working on, complimenting everyone when deadline was met, calling spontaneous meetings to congratulate us on every win, be it a piece of new business or an increase in circulation. Robyn used to joke with the executive management team that we had all thought we were coming to turn the ship around, but in reality we had to raise it from the bottom of the ocean floor.

There were company seminars with behavioural psychologists, including one where Robyn herself had to undergo the terribly confronting 360-degree feedback exercise, when senior management critiqued her performance to her face, but she toughed it out with good grace. Where the company had once been divisive and disjointed, Robyn steered it to a place where every member of staff felt valued and empowered. She had sound business knowledge and editorial understanding. It's a winning combination, especially when you throw in her humour, quick wit and taste.

We once spent a good fifteen minutes at our Monday morning meeting settling on which Royal Doulton tableware we should order for the boardroom, an exercise which I'm sure finance departments would sneer at today. But these details matter when you are creating the *Vogue* culture, because the culture is what you are selling. The thickness of the stationery stock, the flowers on the reception desk, the handwritten thankyou notes, the napkins, the corporate Christmas cards, manners—all of these were an integral part of the brand's DNA, and they were the reason you were charging premium rates for an ad page. Robyn instigated a shared goal of excellence for all, and the sales figures and advertising revenue slowly began to reflect the positive changes. It was an amazing era at Australian Condé Nast. For the rest of my career at *Vogue* I would never again feel so supported and understood by management as I did back then.

There were other superb colleagues, including the inimitable Grant Pearce, who in 1999 held the position of creative services director just prior to his launching the upmarket men's magazine *GQ*. Immensely stylish and charming—and most at home in a bespoke suit with a glass of pinot noir in his hand—Grant had worked at all sorts of jobs in the fashion industry, starting as a storeman and packer at John Kaldor Fabricmakers. Despite his predilection for high-end luxury, and his undoubted skill in this arena, he had a knowledge and appreciation of every area of the fashion industry. He and I became an almost inseparable duo in the marketplace, and he taught me invaluable lessons when it came to interacting with clients.

Grant never over-promised. He would listen to what it was the business required and create a proposition for everybody concerned that was win/win. He was not interested in the dollar for the dollar's sake; he was far more interested in forging relationships that were built on trust and mutual outcomes. He wouldn't agree to anything if he didn't genuinely think it would benefit the client, as well as *Vogue* or *GQ*. He always kept the reader, or the customer, in mind during any deal, because he knew that ultimately they were the most important part of the equation.

After Grant became the publisher of *Vogue*, we had a kind of good-cop, bad-cop routine going where it looked to an outside party that he had to convince me to compromise on certain editorial decisions, but in reality he didn't. I agreed with pretty much everything he suggested because he was nearly always right. He worked hard, he played hard and he was all class. Added to that he was enormous fun to be around. I couldn't have had a better mentor and champion and we had a fantastic partnership that would last more than a decade.

Another central member of the team was events director Sally Bell, who had worked with Robyn for many years at both *Vogue Living* and at Yves Saint Laurent. Sally was another taste-maker, who knew precisely how to put the right layer of gloss and polish on events and promotions. She was also deft at handling PR in what was a very tricky transition period. There were ongoing issues involving Condé Nast and *Vogue* being skewered and gossiped about in the press, a habit that seemed difficult for the journalists to break. My feeling, and it remains so, is that it is dangerous and oftentimes counterproductive to court the press. They really have no interest whatsoever in promoting you—in fact, when it involves an elitist institution such as *Vogue*, it serves them better to lampoon you. They are clever and cynical: you cannot outfox them and they are impossible to impress.

On the few occasions I picked up the phone to complain about something unjust or untrue that was written or aired about myself or the company, I also discovered—most bizarrely—that no one will claim responsibility for how it got in there in the first place. Apparently there are a whole bunch of furtive sub-editors who write and publish the paper while no one is looking. As the editor of *Vogue* I had to take the rap for everything, even a missing comma. My tactic was to just steer clear of them and if by some miraculous circumstance the press happened to write something positive or complimentary, send them flowers and pray to God you were off the hook for another six months.

Any request to comment on models and female body image, which was frequent, was also a disaster poised to happen. The reality of that situation is difficult to defend, and the media, especially television, already have their minds made up about how negatively they intend to portray you. It was better to make no comment, endure the attack, and let them run with the story until it got tired.

In general, the media are interested in maintaining the myth that if you edit a fashion magazine you are a privileged, pampered air-head, or as in the case of, say Anna Wintour, a she-devil. It comes with the gig. You have to develop a very thick skin. On one occasion a

Vogue sub-editor resigned to move interstate, and a newspaper gossip column ran a piece the next day that said: 'Perhaps Clements should stop worrying about what to wear to work and start managing her staff better.' Normally I would ignore this level of crap, but for some reason the inane lack of reason and pettiness really riled me. I called the journalist, who predictably replied that he didn't know how it got in there, despite the fact he edited the page. I told him that if he just let me get on with my job and not target *Vogue* or me, I would never ask him for one sentence of promotion in the paper. It actually worked out perfectly, and the bad press largely subsided.

What you would hope would come with the gig was the secret formula for a winning cover, but that, unfortunately, is one of the biggest mysteries in publishing. Over time, I would learn the hard way what definitely doesn't work, but a successful cover is, in the end, a throw of the dice. In most cases, if you set out to shoot a specific cover and have a preconceived idea about it, you won't be able to make it happen. The team will feel the pressure and something about the resultant image will feel forced. The best approach is to plan that the cover will come from a predetermined shoot and then hope that one of the images will stand out and shout 'cover'.

There is also an overriding pressure from celebrity publicists and model agencies that if their talent is booked for a potential cover it will be a definite. If agreed to, you can find yourself in the unhappy position of being obliged to run a substandard or inappropriate shot because the cover was promised. Our way to circumvent this was to promise a 'cover try', but in current times that doesn't fly anymore. Once magazine editors called all the shots, but the power balance has shifted.

In 2000, the cult of celebrity was at an all-time high, with magazines such as *In Style*, with their star-studded focus gaining huge ground in the marketplace. I quickly found celebrity wrangling to be enervating, exasperating and at odds with what I thought *Vogue* represented. The Hollywood agents are such a powerful force: they would demand to choose the photographer, the location, the hair and makeup artists, and sometimes even the stylist. They would provide a list of designers that could be contacted for clothes, a list of what not to ask the celebrity in question, and then insist on sitting in on the interview. Of course, they expected to see and sanction the piece before it went to print, including layout. We were there merely to organise it and to pay for it all, along with the attendant car services, assistant manicurists, production companies and five-star organic caterers. If an invoice arrived for an astrologer and a dog minder, I wouldn't have been surprised. There were so many hidden palms to be greased. Our overall contribution was that we could print and distribute a manufactured puff piece for them—lucky us. I didn't see the value, neither financially nor creatively. You would need a caffeine patch to get through the simpering copy that was produced as a result of all the sanctions on the talent by their managers.

This was not the case however, when dealing with the Australian celebrities, who were always a pleasure to deal with, understood our budget constraints, and were fully prepared to take the fashion journey with *Vogue*. I made the decision to focus on models, especially the top local girls, and Australian actresses.

A major dilemma I needed to address however, was talent exclusivity. Being *Vogue*, it was imperative that we showcased the best Australian models, but given that the market is small, the girls were appearing everywhere. Alyssa Sutherland was a long-time *Vogue* model, but in one week I noticed her in a rival fashion magazine, a Sunday newspaper colour supplement, and an advertisement for a shopping centre that ran on the side of a bus.

In order to ensure *Vogue* looked like a *Vogue*, I had to guarantee that the top talent in the country, including photographers and writers, aligned themselves with us exclusively. It was a necessary positioning exercise. My stipulation was that our chosen contributors could not work for any rival magazine or supplement (excluding the indie magazines like *Oyster* and *Russh*) unless I gave approval beforehand. It was a tough demand and it did limit editorial opportunities for certain people. I'm forever grateful that model agencies such as Vivien's, Chic and Chadwicks saw the value in aligning their talent with *Vogue*. Dear Susie Deveridge from Vivien's Models would sometimes call me almost in tears after a barrage of complaints from another editor, but she always held firm, and thus we showed loyalty in return by consistently featuring girls like Gemma Ward, Nicole Trunfio and Codie Young.

Photographer Richard Bailey also maintained his lifelong allegiance to *Vogue*, and was our number one go-to guy. He never demanded a formal contract; our understanding was that he would always be given a main-page story per issue, and we worked that way harmoniously for a decade. Richard made an enormous contribution to the rebuilding of *Vogue*: always loyal, always professional. Widely considered to be Australia's top photographer, he could be difficult and sometimes stubborn, but he was also dedicated and he delivered. He was a much-loved member of *Vogue*'s creative family and, even after a diagnosis of cancer which tragically proved to be terminal, he worked tirelessly for the magazine until he died in 2010.

The January 2000 issue was to be the official relaunch of *Vogue Australia*, and I had hired two young women to work on the redesign, Natasha Hasemer and Zoe Pollitt, who had established their own design firm called Eskimo. The cover, of actress/model Mila Jovovich wearing Prada, was shot by my long-time friend Patric Shaw, who had now moved to New York. I loved the attitude that Mila expressed: she looked knowing and confident and sexy. It was exactly the feeling I wanted for the new-look *Vogue*. When the issue appeared on the stands I was thrilled when one of my long-time magazine idols, Lisa Wilkinson, sent me a note congratulating me on the cover. Lisa understood the mood I wanted to project.

What makes the perfect cover is amorphous; the quest for it, relentless. So much can go wrong: models can fall through, the photographer may not capture the exact moment, the clothes could get held up in customs and not arrive, the light may fail, the hair and makeup can turn out badly. Sometimes you were reduced to working with an image that you knew deep down was not quite right, but it was all you had. Because budgets were so tight, I could not drop or 'kill' shoots that I had paid for, so the best compromise had to be found in all situations. On the occasions we could not make our own material work, a lifted shot had to be found.

Producing a good cover that also sells well every month is an editor's greatest stress. Because everybody—and I mean everybody—has an opinion and is not afraid to share it. Every person is an expert. If it sells, they knew it was the right decision. If it doesn't, you won't be able to find them. In the early years covers were chosen by the editor and art director, with plenty of input from the fashion director. It was then shown to management because, in the case of Robyn Holt or

Nancy Pilcher, I respected their opinion. A few years down the track more and more people became involved in cover decisions: circulation managers, marketing departments, publishers and advertising sales teams, each who came with their own largely unproven theories. I knew the major pitfalls to avoid—no black-and-white, no sepia, nothing too brown-toned. No dark backgrounds, nothing too dramatic or depressing. No bikinis (my personal theory is that covergirls in skimpy swimsuits make women feel fat). The subject needed to look glamorous, yet approachable; super-chic, but not too haughty. Happy but not deliriously so. Not overly made up, not wearing fur. Slim, but not too skinny. There was also the chance that the celebrity you were featuring may polarise readers. Gwyneth: love her or hate her? Angelina: haute beauty or home-wrecker? In addition, you had to listen to the breathless research findings with an interested face. Cover lines about hair really sell. The colour pink works on a masthead. Readers react to numbers like '678 hot new looks'. Women like words such as 'shoes'. It's brain-numbing.

This was after you had dealt with the photographers, who wanted everything to look like *Vogue Italia*, which is in a class all of its own and in my mind, inimitable. It's pretentious to even think to mimic it. And it would be a kiss of death in Australia, sales-wise.

If I was unsure of a cover, or on the rare occasion that there was actually more than one choice, I would vox pop it around the office, asking the opinion of the personal assistants and those who had no involvement in either editorial or advertising. But too many opinions just start to confuse the situation. The feedback would start with, 'She looks more pretty on option A', 'I like what she has on on option B', 'I think the yellow type is fresh', to: 'She looks like the bitch that stole my boyfriend.' You can't get consensus.

I remember an art assistant saying to me once: 'Stop asking. If you mix all colours together you end up with brown.' Much later, I felt the same way about querying readers for their opinion on Facebook, or printing covers on the website and asking them to choose. A title such as *Vogue* should lead the market, and offer what we think to be the best. Research is valuable, but an assured *Vogue* is directional. I was always thankful to hear what a reader hated, but in the end I felt it was up to us to inspire. I would be guided by my art director, fashion director and one or two members of the editorial team and that was enough. If the issue bombed, I was prepared to assume total responsibility. I'd have to anyway. There was no phantom sub I could blame.

We saw some small circulation gains in the first twelve months of relaunch, but it was more a halting of the decline. The overall goal was to achieve consistency in an attempt to win back the readers' trust. Condé Nast International Chairman Jonathan Newhouse had been out to visit, and gave me some generally positive feedback about the magazine. I was still finding my feet, and was happy to listen to his critique. Jonathan had made so many trips to Australia during the last two disastrous regimes that he was thoroughly sick to death of the place. He had reportedly clocked up millions of unwanted frequent flyer miles.

During lunch at a restaurant in North Sydney, I politely asked him what he expected from me. Would he like a weekly report, a monthly report? 'Nothing,' he replied. 'As long as everything is going alright, I never want to hear from you and you won't hear from me.' Over the next thirteen years he would contact me only once to comment favourably on a big circulation increase. He never flew to Australia again.

* * *

The first three years spent turning *Vogue* around were arduous and exhausting, but above all, exhilarating. There was so much work to be done and we were all forging and experiencing the dynamics of a completely new team. The art department went through various changes of staff, as did the magazine's design itself, until I employed a witty New Yorker called Paul Meany who hailed from an advertising background. He and I shared very similar tastes and influences, and I felt *Vogue* really start to take shape.

When I reflect, it took me almost three years to hit my stride. By then, the circulation gains were steady, as were ad sales, and the negative press had abated. It is, of course, a far easier task to reinvigorate something that is moribund, rather than trying to improve a product that is already good. Thankfully, the audience gave us time. In today's social media environment, no one would indulge a magazine brand by waiting three years for it to really excel. Nowadays you have about two or three months' grace or the reader will simply cancel their subscription and launch their own superior fashion blog—if they don't already have one.

One of the bonuses of working for Condé Nast was attending the biannual conferences which, in keeping with the values of the company, were held in the world's most glamorous hotels and destinations, such as the Hôtel Du Cap-Eden-Roc in France, the Villa D'Este in Lake Como and the Çirağan Palace Kempinksi in Istanbul.

The first conference I was invited to attend was in 2001, and took place at the luxurious Hotel Cipriani in Venice. Every *Vogue* and *GQ* editor and all the senior executives from around the world were in attendance, excluding the US, which is run separately to Condé Nast International. The pressure (self-imposed at any rate) to pack correctly was enormous.

Nancy and I had a theory that it's impossible to pack for Europe when you're in Australia, especially considering the seriously fashionable party we were about to join. You always take the wrong shoe, and your winter coat will look at least one season out of fashion and smell like mothballs. Because we flew the furthest distance we were able to check-in one day before the rest of the group arrived, and we took the opportunity to race to the nearest Prada store and panic shop. I distinctly recall buying a silk, Prada lipstick-kiss print shirt that was straining over my bust because they only had one left and it wasn't exactly my size.

At one of the lavish Palazzo dinners I was seated next to future fashion icon Anna Dello Russo, who is fun and super bright, and the then publisher of Paris *Vogue*, Gardner Bellanger, an American dynamo with a rapier wit, who I found to be rather fabulous. At one of the daytime conference sessions, the then editor-in-chief of Italian *GQ* was speaking on the subject of what makes an Italian man special. He was quite handsome, with a gravelly, sexy voice, and I suggest most of the women in the room were listening rather intently. Gardner was wearing dark sunglasses and at the end of his speech she leaned forward, and spoke into the microphone on the desk: 'I live in France,' she drawled. 'And you know what we say there: a Frenchman is just an Italian man in a very bad mood.'

Most of the conversations at the conference that year were based around the internet and its potential impact on the magazine business, all in the midst of the NASDAQ crash. Back in Australia, Robyn had the foresight to launch *vogue.com.au* with no budget and a staff of two, which saw immediate success, especially with the popularity of the *Vogue* Forum, a chat room where the audience felt comfortable to discuss all manner of subjects under the banner of *Vogue*, not just fashion.

We all certainly felt we were on a forward trajectory of change, and growth. No greater change than when the whole staff was called into the boardroom one morning in 2003 and told by the Condé Nast Asia Pacific President James Woolhouse that the licence had been sold to an Australian community newspaper and magazine group, the Federal Publishing Company (FPC), owned by Michael Hannan.

One of the girls from the fashion office fainted at that moment and had to be led out of the room. It was a very dramatic *Vogue*-style moment, and I should have thought about doing the same thing—but I was secretly too excited about the fact that we were going to relocate offices to the inner city and I wouldn't have to drive over that wretched Harbour Bridge anymore.

9

KING KARL

Shortly after the Condé Nast titles were transferred into the hands of their new owners, FPC, it was conference time again, and this one was held at the magnificent Hôtel du Cap-Eden Roc in the south of France. I went with our new general manager, New Zealander Michael McHugh, and also Robyn Holt, who was in the transition stages of leaving Australia to take the position of managing director of Condé Nast in Russia.

The trip, in a political sense, was somewhat of a challenge for me: on one hand I was travelling with a soon to be ex-managing director who I liked and respected; on the other was a new boss I barely knew who I needed to both include and please. McHugh was a volatile character with a huge passion for magazines, but he had a mercurial approach to staff. At times he respected my opinion and was my greatest champion, at others he was plotting my demise—predominately the latter I later discovered. It was extremely unsettling and probably not something I would allow myself to be put through again, but I loved my job and at the time the best path through was to remain transparent in everything I did and get on with making the magazine successful. 'Managing up' is exhausting, a waste of emotional energy that could be put to better use elsewhere.

After the conference finished, I took the train to stay with Charla Carter, her husband and two children in their beautiful country farmhouse just outside of Avignon. Mourad and the twins arrived from Sydney and we spent a few days cooking and relaxing. One evening, all the boys left us to watch the football at the stadium in Marseille, so Charla and I opened a bottle of red as a chill evening wind, *le mistral*, rolled in and shrieked around the house, *Wuthering Heights* fashion.

I had rehired Charla as a *Vogue* contributor the moment I went back, and we began to throw around some ideas of what we could do to create a high impact issue for December. The magazine was certainly back on track commercially, but I wanted to stretch the possibilities of what we could reach for editorially. I wanted Australian *Vogue* to feel more global.

Although I felt some trepidation about how I would fare with the new management, I had no qualms about the capabilities of my team or what we could potentially do. Charla and I tossed around the idea of a guest editor—Nancy Pilcher had, of course, commissioned the Baz Luhrmann issue in January 1994, and there had been various guest editorships of magazines such as Paris *Vogue* in the past, but it was not a practice that was prolific. So who would our dream guest editor be?

I think I was on red wine number four when I said grandly: 'Karl Lagerfeld.'

Obviously Lagerfeld is a legendary fashion designer and the master who heads Chanel, but his genius also stretched out to so many other areas. He could write, he could illustrate, he could take the photographs: Karl Lagerfeld's talents are unparalleled.

This made him the perfect candidate, because to have someone genuinely guest edit an issue they have to be able to turn their hand to more than one discipline. Otherwise, it is really you editing the issue and they are just contributing. That can be just as fun and impactful, and it was a format we followed later with Kylie Minogue. But for a comprehensive edit Lagerfeld was the obvious choice, as he is a true Renaissance man. 'But c'mon, as if he would do *Vogue Australia*,' I said glumly. 'Well, I know Eric Pfrunder, the Directeur de l'image for Chanel and close confidente of Karl's. Why don't I just ask?' said Charla chirpily. Charla is always relentlessly upbeat and positive. We opened another bottle and got carried away with all the things we could ask Karl to contribute. In truth, I never thought there was even a remote chance that it would happen.

A week or so later I was back in Sydney when Charla telephoned from Paris. 'Kirstie, you won't believe this. I had an initial conversation with Eric and he didn't knock it on the head. I have to meet with him in a few days' time and he's going to talk to Karl.' I was stunned. I mentioned it to the editorial team, with a 'don't get your hopes up' caveat, and then I heard from Charla. Yes. It was on. Karl was actually keen to do it.

This was 2003, and Karl had not yet extended himself into the myriad of editorial projects that he does today. It was a huge triumph for *Vogue Australia*. When the news leaked around town that he was going to guest edit the December issue, quite a few people refused to believe it.

We immediately started to plan the issue, with Charla as our intermediary woman on the ground in Paris. The long periods of silence in between communications were excruciating for me. Being an Aries and having been on a monthly deadline for most of my working life, I like things to just get done. I like a quick decision, a quick meeting, and for everyone to get moving, fast. I get frustrated with too many last-minute changes. While a magazine does have to have a percentage of its content ready to adjust or move for reasons that are unavoidable, I like to keep that ratio to about 15 to 20 per cent, not 100 per cent. Last-minute changes are one thing; last-minute panics are another, because that's when poor decisions can be made. As an editor, you owe it to your team to be organised. A smooth production flow creates happy staff. And I've always found happy staff far easier to manage.

But this was Karl Lagerfeld and obviously we were going to do things his way. He was busy and largely uncontactable because he chose not to use the telephone or email. His preferred method of correspondence was handwritten notes that he would then fax. I adored it, as he has the most beautiful handwriting and I was receiving personal faxes from *the* Karl Lagerfeld for goodness sake. But they were infrequent to say the least. We were flying blind to a degree.

We knew that he wanted to photograph fashion on Cate Blanchett, Nicole Kidman and Kylie Minogue. That he was willing to shoot a story featuring Australian-only designer fashion. There were also ideas around Australian industrial designer, Marc Newson. And Karl himself perhaps wanted to fly to Australia. But each day, the ideas and the dates changed. Karl is impulsive and capricious, which is a large part of his charm. He is also—let's face it—rather busy. We let Charla take care of the day-to-day communications with Karl in Paris, while we hunkered down and created some ideas of our own.

One of *Vogue*'s greatest assets was editorial and production coordinator Kimberley Walsh. Kimberley had the tenacity and determination of a pitbull, all delivered with a level of professionalism and sweetness that is completely disarming. Kimberley, Leigh Ann Pow and I began working together in 1999 and they were both there until the end, thirteen years later. I cannot imagine having done my job without them. Kimberley had one of those driver/driver personalities that are calculated in a Myers-Briggs test, but I think there should have been a different category for her because she never, ever gave up. She was always fiercely protective of me, given that she also triple-billed as my PA, but she was very protective of the brand too.

We could sense this Karl edition was going to be a logistical challenge, both in planning and in execution—but what an exciting ride. We had to make deadline. And stay on budget. No stress.

Kimberley, Leigh Ann and I began to work on back-up contingency plans, and the team devised 'turn pages' (the editorial that appears at the front of the magazine, before you get to the fashion spreads) that were Karl- or Chanel-related so that we could at least have something completed if concepts fell through. As we brainstormed each turn, whether it was Karl-inspired white shirts, or Chanel jewellery pages, we duly sent them to Karl for his personal sign-off.

Michael McHugh was thoroughly on board with the project and just as eager as I was to make it all happen. Lunches were immediately organised in Sydney and Melbourne to let our advertising clients know about the upcoming issue. At a lunch at The Stokehouse in St Kilda, Melbourne, I delivered a short speech about how amazed and honoured I was to have someone like Karl Lagerfeld guest editing *Vogue Australia*, and what a unique collaboration it would be.

After I sat down at the table, a junior media buyer from an advertising agency who was seated opposite, and looked to be about twenty years old, picked up his vintage Moët & Chandon and eyeballed me, clearly unimpressed. 'What are you going to do for the *Vogue* readers who don't know who Karl Lagerfeld is? For example, I don't,' he smirked, as if he was slapping down a trump card. I had no answer. He was simply following the ignorant and ungenerous Australian tradition of refusing to be impressed by anyone or anything, even one of the world's greatest living fashion designers. It's moments like these when you appreciate what your ad team has to contend with on a daily basis. It took all my self-control not to snatch the champagne out of his hand. Or at least start serving him domestic.

Karl and I were on the same wavelength about which Australian celebrities we would have contribute, starting with the exceptional Cate Blanchett. His concept was to photograph Cate portraying Mme Coco Chanel, so the shoot was set in the Rue Cambon boutique, Chanel's private apartment, and in the surrounding cafés and streets of Paris. Cate was working in London at the time, and had jumped at the idea. Charla was also well acquainted with Cate, as they had worked together on previous occasions, including on a cover for *Vogue Australia*, so the logistics were relatively smooth.

In the first part of the series, Cate poses as the designer; in the second part, she is presented as a young, modern woman, wearing and being fitted with Chanel couture. Cate was completely transformed. It remains perhaps my very favourite Australian *Vogue* shoot, not only for the famous talents that were involved but for the timelessness and sheer drama of the photographs.

Cate Blanchett and *Vogue Australia* have had a long and close relationship over the years, beginning with her first appearance in the magazine as 'One to Watch' when she graduated from NIDA in 1992. During the Marion Hume period at *Vogue* in 1997, I was sent to style Cate for a feature story. At the time, she was in the midst of filming her breakthrough film *Elizabeth*, which would garner her the Golden Globe for Best Actress and also an Academy Award nomination. I had Valentino dresses that had been sent from Italy, and we were laughing because she was in character and thus had very visible leg and underarm hair. Richard Bailey thought it was fantastic, so in one of the pictures Cate deliberately raised her arm to juxtapose her unshaven armpits against the couture sheath.

Over the years, we worked together for *Vogue* on numerous occasions and she was always incredibly professional, calm and focused on getting the best results. Cate loves the grandeur of costume and corsets, and would bring a sense of drama and gravitas to the photoshoots. But only for the shot. In person, she is a lovely, low-maintenance person. She clicked with Richard Bailey, and at the wrap of a long day she would sometimes have her children drop by the studio so they could have a family portrait taken together. We considered her part of the *Vogue* family; however, she always maintained a sense of polite distance. She's there to get the job done, simple as that.

Other collaborations in the issue included Kylie Minogue, whom Karl photographed wearing Chanel and cavorting on his piano at his home in Paris. Kylie was also more than happy to participate. It doesn't matter how big a star you are, everybody wants to be in Karl's orbit.

I was also in negotiations with Nicole Kidman, who was high on Karl's wish list. This was not uncommon: oftentimes during my career, I was in negotiations regarding Nicole Kidman, most of them fruitless. I started to sense that Nicole's management had a strategy in place which meant she would be available to shoot for *Harper's Bazaar Australia* but only allow *Vogue Australia* to lift other material that had been produced for international *Vogue* editions. I can see that this plan certainly saved Nicole's time and energy, but it didn't save mine, because for years I had conversations with her agent Wendy Day about the possibility of us shooting her that would drag on for months and never eventuate.

On this particular occasion it began on a vaguely positive note, but then became more and more convoluted. Nicole would be in New York; no, she would be in London; yes, maybe Paris; no, no, in an unspecified location. At one point I thought I almost had her on a jet, or in a helicopter, or a spaceship, or something, going to Karl's home in Biarritz for a half-day shoot, and then no, it all fell away again. Added to this was the difficulty of making a date work in Karl's diary, who was not idle or unimportant himself.

Baz Luhrmann had been commissioned to fly to Biarritz to conduct a one-on-one interview with Karl for the issue. This article would give a wonderful and piercingly honest insight into Karl, his career, and his complicated relationship with his mother. Shortly afterwards I became aware that Karl and Baz were also talking about a future collaboration on a short promotional film for Chanel No. 5, starring—who would have predicted—Nicole Kidman. And yet, Karl's people were asking me every day how far I'd got with pinning a date down with her.

Wendy Day was now suggesting that we fly Karl and his entire photographic retinue to New York for a day with Nicole. Given that Karl travels by private jet and with a major domo, for starters, I feigned breathless excitement over the phone while mentally calculating the preposterous cost of sending God knows how many people to NYC for a possible one-day shoot. No more faxes. I needed to speak to Karl.

After days and days of wrangling we eventually settled on a time for him to call. I was at a Diesel dinner at the Overseas Passenger Terminal in Sydney when finally my mobile sounded. I rushed outside and stood on the wharf in the moonlight looking at the Opera House when Karl came on the line. Friendly and enthusiastic, he talked about how much he was enjoying working on the issue, and how he hoped to come to Sydney for the launch. I politely suggested that he should take over the Nicole Kidman negotiations because I was certain he had more pull, and he told me—not unlike a kindly uncle—to leave it with him. We agreed to meet during the Paris RTW collections in the coming weeks to finalise details and conduct the cover shoot. Karl Lagerfeld had basically just given me a 'Don't worry Kirstie, everything's going to be fine' pep talk. It was another one of my pinch-me moments.

The cover was always going to be problematic though. I absolutely could not have two stars as big as Cate Blanchett and Nicole Kidman in one issue and choose one over the other to be on the cover. Their agents had made that perfectly plain from the outset, and if we were to go back on our word we would have hell to pay. I made the bird-in-the-hand decision of completing the Cate Blanchett shoot first. I would worry about Nicole afterwards.

Leigh Ann always spent a large percentage of her working life being tortured by Hollywood agents, often being called in Sydney at 3 a.m. for some insane request to be addressed, such as who was going to meet the 'star' at the kerb at Heathrow airport when the hire car pulled up and then walk them to the first-class check in? When you are dealing with famous celebrities you have to toughen up and play the game. The Karl issue was no walk in the park, but we'd had worse on other occasions. There was one unspeakably obnoxious LA agent we used to call the 'raw nerve'. Anytime we had to deal with her, we would be compelled to have a cup of tea and take ten deep breaths in my office afterwards, before we went home to hug our children.

Karl's timetable was too crowded for him to make a visit to Australia while he was making the issue, so it was decided that he would instead dispatch his friend Hedi Slimane, the designer of Dior Homme (now the creative director of Saint Laurent), to contribute. We were all huge fans of Hedi Slimane, and his brief was to explore Sydney and produce his own personal photographic essay.

We booked him into the penthouse suite at Blue, in Woolloomooloo, and I went to meet him for a cup of tea on the wharf one dazzlingly sunny morning. Slimane had never been to Australia, and admitted to a large degree of trepidation over travelling such a long way from Paris. He was a quiet, gentle person who seemed either shy, or perhaps not interested in talking just for the sake of it. As we were discussing what he intended to do during his stay, an enormous flock of cockatoos flew in, landed on the wharf near our table and began screeching at each other raucously. Slimane, who couldn't have looked more out of place in his David Bowie, *Man Who Fell To Earth*-way, whippet-thin with a black Dior Homme jacket, perfect white shirt and bowl haircut, looked at me in utter amazement and said: 'Does this always happen?'

Slimane was very easy to entertain for his week-long stay, requesting only a car and driver, and a camera. He had his own contacts, and mainly wanted to hang out with skaters and musicians, so we sent him off to Ksubi headquarters to meet the cool kids and told him to call us if he needed anything. He didn't. He called one morning and said he would like to meet with Paul Meany, the magazine's art director, so I gave him the address of the office and didn't tell the staff he was coming. It was fun walking into the fashion office and saying, 'Hi girls, have you meet Hedi Slimane by the way?' Everybody was beside themselves, but he was so natural and unassuming. His photographic essay was a very personal take on Sydney, a series of black-and-white portraits of youth subculture, displaying his signature sense of grungy realism.

My next step was to organise for Paul Meany, Charla and myself to meet with Karl in Paris, so we could discuss the rest of the issue. The meeting was held at 7L in the Rue de Lille, which is the address of Karl's photographic studio and which also has a large bookstore facing the streetfront. He was late, but we were installed in the studio and enjoying ourselves immensely, delving into the piles and piles of art and photography books that were stacked around the room. There was a shoot being set up for another magazine, and streams of people were dashing in and out, one being the English aristocrat and Chanel muse Lady Amanda Harlech, who was absolutely charming and self-deprecating. Karl's personal chef was in the kitchen off to the side and kept sending out the most delicious appetizers for us to nibble on while we waited.

Finally, in the late afternoon, Karl appeared with his goblet of Pepsi Max on a silver tray. Paul and I were understandably nervous but he could not have been more welcoming and understated. He was fast and funny, and we spent the first few minutes talking about his new iPod, which was oh-so-new in 2003. Just as impressive was the case he had that contained 36 iPods, each of which he claimed was at capacity. Obviously there was a full-time employee to do the syncing.

Karl has immense charisma. The air crackles when he arrives. He is the opposite of aloof, and can switch from German to English to French in mid-sentence, while being witty and erudite in all of them.

If I had a wish where I could invite any ten people in the world to a dinner party, I'd simply just invite him.

We flicked though a number of books on his table and Karl indicated that he admired the work of the moody Australia photographer Bill Henson, so it was decided that we would ask him to contribute a portfolio to the issue, which he ultimately did. That was a first for any fashion publication in Australia.

Karl then very generously invited us all to join him for a private lunch at his home on the Rue de l'Universite later that week. As I picked myself up off the floor and hurriedly accepted, Charla said, 'Oh, damn, I can't. I have a freelance job.' Karl just laughed and said, 'No, no, I get it. We all have to make a living.'

Paul and I were so excited on the day of the proposed lunch I think we arrived about half an hour early and had to circle the block a number of times. At the appointed hour we were ushered through the main dining room of his beautiful 18 000 square foot *hôtel particulier*, which was adorned with the most spectacular floral centrepiece. Karl emerged and explained that there was to be a formal dinner that evening, and a TV show taping that afternoon, so he was being a very grand 'Karl'. Eric Pfrunder joined us and we moved into a smaller 'breakfast' room, adjacent to the dining room and overlooking the garden, furnished with eccentric German and Viennese ceramics, lamps and furniture from the late nineteenth and early twentieth centuries.

Lunch was easy and convivial, and even though Karl was on his very strict diet, the food was sensational. I mentioned that we had just been to see a wonderful exhibition of Marlene Dietrich's personal wardrobe. Karl had known her and said he couldn't stand her, and made some salacious and hilarious comments, best not repeated.

He knew Marlene Dietrich! I was overawed. When Paul and I tumbled onto the street a couple of hours later, it took a few minutes for us to compose ourselves. It was a once in a lifetime experience.

We immediately caught the Metro over to the 16th and Paul bought a Dior Homme tuxedo worth two months' pay to celebrate, but he had decided he must have something to wear to the launch party.

My next rendezvous with Karl was scheduled during the Milan collections, which were due to start the following week. We met at the Fendi showroom the evening before the show, and I sat at the desk with him, watching with fascination as each exit was brought out for his tweaking and approval.

He was in a somewhat mischievous mood and had tired of the long negotiations with Nicole Kidman. 'You know, I saw a photo of the model Eva Herzigová in a magazine and she looks just like Nicole!' he exclaimed. 'Why don't we shoot Eva wearing couture and we can have her doing all Nicole's red carpet poses? We can have a little fun with it.' That is exactly what we did. It solved both my cover and budget problems. We could put Cate on the cover, or a model. There would be no Hollywood agent stand-off.

The shoot with Eva was held at 7L late one afternoon and we shot well into the night. Amanda Harlech was there again, and US *Vogue*'s contributing editor André Leon Talley dropped by to watch. Eva is so glamorous and a consummate model. She was mostly glued to her mobile phone all evening, and from what I could discern she is fluent in more than half a dozen languages. When she admired the gorgeous black Dior Homme overcoat Karl was wearing (in French), he promptly draped it over her bare shoulders and gave it to her. The Nicole Kidman homage was our little tongue-in-cheek secret, and I don't think anyone in the Australian press (or Nicole's agent Wendy Day) picked up on it, but every one of Eva's poses were copied from Kidman's past red carpet appearances.

Getting the issue to the printers on time was a massive challenge for the entire staff, but Karl came through like the professional he is, just in the nick of time. We certainly had some nail-biting moments when we were waiting on elements, such as his approval of Paul's layouts, but the emergency plans we had put in place meant that we could always progress with at least some pages and in the end it all came together.

We then began to plan a massive launch party, which we decided to hold at the Sydney Opera House, choosing a suitably famous landmark to celebrate a most momentous occasion. Karl had expressed interest in attending right up until the very end, and we had booked hotels and started to lose sleep over details like chauffeurs, restaurants, bodyguards, weather, everything. Our events director Sally Bell was magnificent. The invitations, with a fold-out silhouette of Karl, designed by Paul Meany, were dispatched and the buzz around town was 'would he or wouldn't he be there?' Then we received the devastating news that, due to overlapping commitments and the great distance, Karl would not be able to travel to Sydney. He promised however (I think to assuage my disappointment), he would record a video message to play on the night.

The event planning went ahead, and then one afternoon Sally appeared at the door of my office. 'Look what I've got,' she said in her lilting Scottish accent, shaking a video tape. It was Karl's recording. We rushed into the boardroom and watched Karl descend regally down his staircase at his home, pause at the bottom, and speak about how much he enjoyed editing *Vogue Australia*, working with me and how he dearly wished he could be at the party with us all. Sally and I burst into tears.

The party was expensive, chic and swank, filled to capacity with elegantly dressed guests sipping on icy champagne and delicious canapés. Michael McHugh spoke, I spoke, and we ran Karl's video. Charla flew out from Paris, there were fireworks on the harbour, and placed on tables around the room were the very first advance copies of the December 2003 issue, guest edited by Karl Lagerfeld. It had been a marvellous, unforgettable rollercoaster.

The next day I scanned the papers to read the social pages. And the only mention I could find centred on the fact that the writer couldn't help sniggering at the video because Karl, apparently, resembled a Thunderbird puppet.

10

A PRINCESS DIARY

There are some stories that are irresistible to an editor. I had been keeping my eye on the burgeoning romance between a young Australian woman, Mary Donaldson, and Frederik, Crown Prince of Denmark, who met at the Slip Inn during the Sydney Olympics in 2000. The story went that apparently not wanting to reveal his profile, the prince introduced himself to Mary as Fred. They fell head over heels in love. I noted that there were trips back and forth to Denmark and Sydney for the two of them, until it was reported that at the end of 2001 Mary had quietly moved to Denmark. It was obvious that the relationship was serious, and that she was perhaps 'in training' for the next stage.

It was a real-life fairytale, every woman's fantasy of becoming a princess, even for a cynical republican such as myself. Editorial co-ordinator Kimberley Walsh was obsessed with Mary. She had a 'Mary' file on her desktop and she would scan the internet for shots of her every morning. Kimberley, Leigh Ann and I were looking at some Mary photographs one morning over tea, musing over how daunting the royal grooming lessons might be when I said, 'She's probably homesick. Let's send her a *Vogue Australia* subscription.' Leigh found the palace contact details and Kimberley eagerly wrapped our latest issue in white tissue paper, tied it with a *Vogue* ribbon and airfreighted it to Mary. Every single month.

Sometimes I would pop a handwritten card inside, other times not. It just became a monthly ritual, and meanwhile Leigh Ann also began to make polite enquires through the official palace channels about a possible *Vogue* article.

This went on for over a year when finally the engagement was announced in October 2003. Leigh Ann intensified her campaign with no definite word either way coming back from palace officials. The royal wedding was held in May 2004, and attracted nation-wide attention in Australia. Most weddings leave me dry-eyed, but the story behind this couple accidently finding love in an ordinary Aussie pub was catnip to me as a journalist.

Several months before the wedding I had travelled to Copenhagen with the Danish luxury house Georg Jensen to join a press tour of their atelier and attend a gala dinner held in the National Gallery. My great friend fashion scribe Tim Blanks was also on the trip, and one chilly afternoon we were treated to a daytime harbour cruise and a visit to the Amalienborg Palace complex, a large square in central Denmark flanked by four palaces.

The Changing of the Guard had just begun, so Tim and I jostled our way to the front to watch the proceedings. I stared up at one of the palace balconies and imagined Mary somewhere inside, taking Danish lessons. 'You know,' I said to Tim, 'there's a beautiful Tasmanian girl called Mary who is set to wed the Crown Prince. I want that story for *Vogue* soooo bad.' Tim, in his usual glib manner said, 'Are you having an "it should have been me" moment Kirst?' Admittedly I was caught up in the whole romantic dream, but more than anything I wanted to be in that palace, interviewing Mary. 'I am going to get the story, believe me,' I said to Tim as we readjusted our scarves in the freezing wind and headed back to the boat.

* * *

By the time the royal wedding was over, Kimberley's Princess Mary obsession had taken on biblical proportions. Leigh Ann had continued to valiantly email the palace, but then we decided to get serious and ramp it up a notch. We wrote an email to Mary, suggesting that this was the ideal time to capture her as she embarked on her journey as the Princess of Denmark; we would create a photographic marking of this new, remarkable stage in her life. We dropped top photographer's names like no tomorrow. We heard nothing.

Then, one Friday about 6 p.m., I was in my office gathering my things to go home. The rest of the team had left for the weekend. I glanced at my watch and realised that now was the ideal hour to call Denmark. Leigh Ann had tracked down the direct line to the Lord Chamberlain, so I dialled his number with no great sense of expectation that he would even answer. But surprisingly, he did.

I hastily regrouped my thoughts, introduced myself and humbly went through my spiel. Then he said affably, 'Ah hello. Yes. I know about this. I spoke to the princess this morning. She said yes, she would like to do it.'

Much like when the doctor told me I was having twins, I thought I'd misheard.

'Excuse me?' I stammered, trying to stay composed. 'Did you say, yes, she'll do it?'

'Yes, we just have to work out when,' he replied.

This was unbelievable. Mary had done no interviews, no magazine sittings. They were one of the world's most glamorous, and private, royal couples. This was a *coup nonpareil*.

I recall hanging up and actually screaming 'Yeeessssss!' down an empty office corridor, before I called Leigh Ann and Kimberley to give them the news. I called to let Michael McHugh know, and he also—to his credit—joined in the general hysteria. The project was not going to be cheap, so he would have to sell it to FPC's proprietor Michael Hannan as a huge win for potential circulation.

It was also crucial that we kept it under wraps so as to not spoil the impact when the magazine did come out. I have never felt stress as intently as I did in the lead-up to leaving for Copenhagen, and actually ended up at the doctor's as a result of the anxiety.

When I became the editor of *Vogue* I basically gave up writing, because I felt that I should be the figurehead of the magazine and leave the content to my team. But if a story was particularly topical, or the subject very high profile, I thought it made sense for me to write the piece. I missed writing and Princess Mary was the story I wanted to tell.

I employed fashion stylist Trevor Stones to work on the project; he was already a *Vogue* contributor and we all began working on the logistics. The photographer chosen was Regan Cameron, who would fly in with his team from New York. Princess Mary requested her makeup artist, Soren Hedegaard; a hair stylist, Jonathan Connelly, would come from elsewhere in Europe; and Trevor and I would fly to

Copenhagen from Sydney. It was a very closed set—no manicurists, no manicurists' assistants, no astrologers.

The shoot was planned for September, prior to the RTW shows in Milan. Trevor had asked every designer who sent clothes to agree to complete confidentiality; it was a like a stealth campaign. The night before I was due to leave, Michael McHugh called me at home while I was packing. I thought he was going to wish me luck but instead he asked me if I thought FPC could afford what it was going to cost. He had already seen the budgets and we had kept costs down to the bare minimum. It was a question that would have been better directed towards Michael Hannan, but the call was intended to hand me total responsibility for all consequences—financial and otherwise—right at the eleventh hour. It had been impossible to go to market with the fact that Princess Mary was going to be on the cover, so our advertisers just had to trust we had something special up our sleeve. But this was a once in a lifetime editorial opportunity and I knew it would sell. The conversation just made me more determined to make the project unforgettable.

Trevor and I flew to Copenhagen, checked into the Hotel d'Angleterre, and made contact with our connection to the palace, Princess Mary's personal assistant Anja Camilla Alaidi. Anja was a young, attractive brunette, very cool in her jeans and boots, but all business. That evening the three of us gathered in the bar of the hotel, to meet with photographer Regan Cameron and discuss how events would roll out. The next day I was to interview Princess Mary at the palace, after which Trevor and I were to go through the fashion with her, trying things on so that we could make a preselection, while Regan was to scout the palace for locations. Regan is originally a New Zealander and I had worked with him in the early days at *Vogue Australia*, mostly on beauty shoots when I was an assistant. Since then

Regan had hit the big-time overseas, and he arrived in Copenhagen with some big-time New York attitude.

He strolled into the bar, said hello to everyone, and then declared that he was going back up to his room. 'You can work out things with my assistant,' he said over his shoulder as he departed, while his colleague sat down at the table. Anja looked at me, wide-eyed with disbelief. 'What did he just say?' she glowered. 'Where did he go? No, no, no. We are discussing the Prince and Princess of Denmark!' She rounded on the assistant. 'Go up and get him NOW or the shoot is off.' I adored her for that. Normally that's something I would have to do.

Regan got the message and was back in an instant. He was a pleasure to work with after that.

The following day we were collected from the hotel by palace staff in 4WDs and driven the short distance to the palace of Christian VIII. Trevor and I were so excited we practically skipped up the red-carpeted stairs and were then led to an antechamber, situated off a main ballroom. Protocol had been explained to us: we were to address Mary as Crown Princess Mary, or Your Royal Highness unless she directed us otherwise, and we were not to enter or leave a room before her, or of course any other member of the royal family we may encounter. There was no curtsying although I would have been more than happy to do so; I love all that pomp and ceremony.

Suddenly Mary walked briskly into the room wearing a beige cashmere sweater, pencil skirt and high-heeled pumps, and reached out to shake my hand with a beaming smile. Trevor disappeared and Mary and I sat down at the table to conduct the interview, while we were served afternoon tea. She was open and disarmingly frank, laughed easily and actually seemed to enjoy the interview process. There was only one question she declined to answer, which was: what were the circumstances in which Frederick proposed? On every other issue she was totally candid, and her responses felt genuine to me and not at all rehearsed.

I have a notebook full of our conversation, and when I look at the notes I made it turns out a lot of our conversation didn't make it into the article because we talked for so long. Mary was an exceedingly generous interview subject. I was so jittery at the beginning I was too scared to pick up my porcelain teacup for fear my hands would shake, but after ten minutes I felt like I was chatting with a friend.

Time passed easily, our discussion reached a natural conclusion and then Trevor was back in the room, ready for the fashion run-through. Anja popped in with a jewellery box and laid some pieces out on a sideboard. There's nothing quite like being casually invited by the Princess of Denmark to come and look through the crown jewels with her to see if there is anything we liked. Trevor and I were mute.

Mary has a fantastic figure, and even though many of the pieces we had brought were couture-sizing, they fitted like a glove. She was so sweet that Trevor momentarily forgot she was royal and at one point put his hands on either side of her tiny waist and pronounced: 'You look fabulous, darling.' Swiftly realising his faux pas and sensing that there may have been the possibility of a *Game Of Thrones*-style beheading by Anja, he spun around and looked at me with fear and horror crossing his face simultaneously—but Mary couldn't have cared less.

We said our goodbyes, returned to the hotel, ordered a martini to celebrate the occasion and called Trevor's mum in Wangaratta to discuss every detail of the day's events.

Back in my room I switched on the television to the abject horror that was the aftermath of the Beslan school massacre. I quickly turned it off, and I cancelled the *Herald Tribune*. I needed this week to be a magical fairytale. The grim reality of the world could wait.

During my conversation with Anja in the bar I had casually mentioned that if Prince Frederik would like to drop by the shoot at any stage, well, we'd be thrilled. And obviously, if he would like to be in a photo, I was sure we could accommodate that. We had never mentioned Frederik in any part of our correspondence, but to have him feature in the shoot with his new wife would be major coup and add an even greater sense of intimacy to the portfolio. I played it down like it was no big deal and Anja said she didn't think it would be possible, but to leave it with her.

The following day we all assembled in a massive ballroom inside Christian VII's palace, part of the Amalienborg complex. A hair and makeup station had been set up in the corner, and Soren and Jonathan began to work on Mary. She was friendly and chatty, as were the household staff who would occasionally bustle purposefully around the room. Regan was setting up, and there was little for me to do, so I was wandering around the ballroom when the very laidback housekeeper asked me if I would like to see the present room. This was another grand ballroom, which was piled high with wedding gifts from around the world. It was astonishing. 'Phht,' said the housekeeper. 'This is only about a tenth of it.' She then declared that I needed to visit the Flora Danica room.

Indeed I did. It was a vast room with the walls and cabinets full of the most marvellous Flora Danica china—prestigious Royal Copenhagen porcelain dating from the seventeen-hundreds. At each end of the room were two massive, carved marble basins with enormous gold spouts.

'This is the room where we hold dinner for the Prime Minister. In olden times, those taps would run with wine,' said my guide proudly.

She was a gem. 'You may walk around the palace if you like,' she told me. 'There are some very famous tapestries you should see.' I was left to meander through the palace rooms alone, admiring the art, furniture and antiquities, and the breathtaking historical tapestries cloaking the great walls. It was heaven.

I eventually returned to the main ballroom to check on the team's progress. Regan had set up a large light and Trevor put Mary into her first outfit, a form-fitting black Prada dress. She looked radiant, and it was then we noticed that she was visibly trembling, she was so nervous. She may have wed the Prince of Denmark and become European royalty, but she was still a young woman on her very first *Vogue* shoot and she wanted to do her best. I stood around making encouraging remarks and we began shooting.

During a break in the proceedings I was off in a corner—admiring a footstool or something—when I heard Mary call my name. 'Come over here and watch this,' she said beckoning me over to the window. She opened it and we both leaned out. 'Look, it's the Changing of the Guard.' There I was in Christian VII's palace in Denmark, standing next to Princess Mary, observing the crowd in the square below. The exact square where I had stood with Tim Blanks, a few months previously, looking up and imagining 'what if?' A few people in the crowd caught sight of Mary and waved excitedly. The hairs on the back of my neck stood on end. I could not believe I had actually made it to this place. With an idea, a *Vogue* business card, and a lot of perseverance, my team and I had turned a dream into reality. I think that precise moment may have been the highlight of my entire career.

If I thought the day couldn't get any better, it was just about to. Anja trotted up to me and said, 'Oh, by the way, I spoke to Frederik. He's going to come to the shoot and he will allow you to take one or two photographs. What would you like him to wear?' Trevor and I went into the dressing area and shared a private shriek of joy, before we pulled ourselves together, went back out and said casually: 'Oh, just jeans and a white shirt.' Prince Frederik strode into the room some time afterwards, with a freshly laundered white shirt in dry-cleaning plastic slung over his shoulder, and a portable CD player in the other hand. I hadn't realised he was so handsome. Mary's face lit up when she saw him. Frederik was charm personified. Not only had Mary found her prince, he was gorgeous, sociable and a Navy Seal. She had pretty much won the marriage lottery.

Frederik changed quickly into his shirt, switched on the CD player and walked over to his wife. The sound of BB King filled the ballroom, and the couple began dancing in the sunlight that was streaming through the open window, as if it was the most natural thing in the world. Regan was shooting, furiously intent on capturing the moment, when Frederik leaned in and kissed his wife on the forehead. Trevor and I were losing it at this point. I may have been in tears. It was everything I had hoped for; a private moment between two royals who were very much in love.

We took another shot of the couple outside, arms entwined, and then wrapped for the day. I went to sleep knowing that we already pulled off the most important shots. The rest would be a creative adventure.

The following day we would be shooting outside the city, at Fredensborg Palace, the Queen and Prince Consort's main residence, and where Frederik and Mary were also living. Regan had requested that we have a horse in one of the photos so we made a trip to the Royal Stables to peruse them. It was a kind of horse casting.

I am no equine expert, but I have never seen horses as towering and magnificent as the Danish Royal horses. There were also dozens of sumptuous royal coaches dating back centuries, including tiny children's carriages. I had to be physically dragged away I was so enraptured.

While Trevor, Soren and Jonathan were preparing the princess, I took a stroll around the magnificent gardens and the boathouse with yet another amiable member of the royal staff, who appeared to be the palace caretaker. Queen Margrethe II was in residence, and it was mentioned that she may have been in the Orangery—the huge glasshouse filled with plants—but our directive was to shoot in the gardens and to not enter the main palace.

The caretaker, Regan and I were all standing by a tree chatting when an SUV came into view, pulling behind it a mammoth horse trailer. 'Ah, here is the horse for the photograph. He's a big fellow,' the caretaker said. The horse was clearly not happy about being cooped up, because the trailer began rocking violently as the horse whinnied fierce protests of complaint.

We waited for what seemed a very long time until finally another car arrived and Princess Mary emerged, dressed in a dazzling Jean Paul Gaultier gown, and wearing a large hat topped with a long feather. Now we just needed the horse.

I looked over with fear and trepidation at the heaving trailer. The noise emanating from inside was unsettling. What unearthly beast had they chosen? Fortunately for Mary, she had been a competent horsewoman before she met Frederik. It's a very useful skill to have if you are planning to join a European royal family, as hunting parties are apparently *de rigueur*. The royal equerry was attempting to open the trailer door, which our unseen stallion was, it seemed, attempting to pulverise with his hoofs. The horse burst out, nostrils flaring. In my mind he reared up on his back legs with flames shooting from his mouth, eyes a ferocious yellow, but that may be a tad dramatic. Anyway, he seemed to be about ten metres high and was completely terrifying.

I'm deathly scared of horses—yet another clear indicator that I was never destined to be royal. I immediately ran and hid behind the nearest tree and scrunched my eyes shut. Mary poked her head around my hiding place and laughed. 'Are you frightened of horses, Kirstie?' The horse was bucking and stamping and Princess Mary just walked straight towards him. He was about as welcoming as a firing squad.

I was thinking, 'No, Mary! Don't do it, don't be crushed by a demonic horse, we've got three more shots to get done today!' Even the royal bodyguards—also ironically hiding behind trees—looked a little anxious. But she simply bent her head to him and let him sniff at her hat, until he gradually calmed down. She's not only the Crown Princess of Denmark, she's a horse whisperer.

There were more thrills to come. After the shot with the horse from hell was over, Regan asked for a chair to be placed on the lawn for Mary to sit on. 'What sort of a chair?' enquired the caretaker.

'Well, what do you have?' I asked innocently.

'Why don't you come with me and choose one?' he suggested. We walked up to the main palace and into a smaller building off to the side. He then led me up some stone steps and we arrived at a large door. Once again, I'm going to say he had a huge, rusty skeleton key, but I may be embellishing somewhat. By now I was completely lost in my Hans Christian Andersen storybook world. If Thumbelina had turned up for afternoon tea I wouldn't have been surprised.

He threw open the door and said, 'Here it is. The chair room.' It was a cavernous storage room the size of a ballroom, stacked with chairs, stools and chaise lounges; in mint condition or needing repairs. There were literally hundreds and hundreds of them, their bolts of original upholstery fabrics interspersed throughout the room. This furniture dated back centuries; it had been in the royal palaces stretching back to the beginning of the monarchy. It was simply incredible, the historic resonance of the room. If Tory Collison, with her love of all things antique, had been witness to this treasure trove I'm quite sure she would have fainted.

'Are there other rooms like this?' I gasped. 'Oh yes,' replied the caretaker. 'Ones for tables, china, lamps.' I didn't hear the rest. I was in raptures over a divine eighteenth-century satin ottoman. I've never fully recovered from the thrill of visiting the Danish Royal chair storage room.

The team broke for lunch and Mary invited us to have sandwiches in a room to the side of the kitchen at their private apartments, where we were joined once again by Frederik. It seems absurd to say it felt completely normal to be having lunch and chatting to the Crown Prince and Princess of Denmark at home, but that is how hospitable and down to earth they are. After lunch, Frederik offered to show Regan and me his luxury car collection. Car enthusiasts will be furious with me because I have no interest in cars whatsoever, and cannot remember what undoubtedly spectacular makes and models the prince was proudly pointing out to me, but suffice it to say he has his very own petrol bowser too.

We returned to the gardens in the late afternoon to shoot one more portrait of the princess. Parts of Fredensborg Gardens are open to the public, and when people passed and realised they were seeing the new Crown Princess they waved and grinned madly, especially the children. Mary took it all in her stride, with real humility. 'I didn't really do anything to deserve all this attention,' she had confessed to me in our interview the day before. 'I simply married the man I love.' That afternoon we captured what would turn out to be the cover shot, a candid photo of Mary juxtaposed against the lush autumnal Danish woods, in a royal purple satin dress, pinned at the centre with a brooch from the crown jewels.

After the last shot was taken we were again invited back to the royal couple's residence and Frederik broke out the champagne to toast the success of the shoot. I didn't want the experience to end. Thanks to the power of *Vogue*, I had been transported into a rarefied world of great wealth and privilege yes, but also of great generosity.

The following week I was back on the regular circuit, attending the RTW fashion shows in Milan. In the evenings I sat by the open window in my tiny hotel room, transcribing and writing my article. On the first day of the shows I was seated next to Judith Cook, who had now become the fashion director of *In Style* magazine. The Princess Mary project was still under wraps but I couldn't contain myself. Judith would understand the intensity of what I had just experienced in Denmark. I told her where I'd just been, she grabbed my arm and we both got goosebumps. She was the perfect person to share the achievement with.

Princess Mary and I continued to liaise for several weeks afterwards, as she had to approve the photographs and my story. She made no changes to the piece and was very happy with all of the photographs, bar one where she thought her face looked strange. It didn't, but Mary had her doubts and wouldn't give it her sign-off. Deadline was upon us and I needed to push it through. Mary and I went back and forth on email and by phone. We retouched the shot and tried again, but she was still resisting. One afternoon I was on my way home when my mobile rang. It was Mary. 'Hello Princess Mary,' I said as I pulled the car over to the side of the road in suburban Kingsford. It felt slightly incongruous, chatting to a princess while driving down busy Gardeners Road.

'I still don't like the photograph. It doesn't look like me,' she said. I disagreed, politely of course. 'I'm fixated on it, aren't I?' she laughed. 'Just tell me to be quiet and get over it.' So I told the Crown Princess of Denmark that she needed to trust me and get over it. And she relented.

The December 2004 issue, featuring Mary on the cover in the purple satin dress, wearing the royal crown jewels, was a spectacular success and a complete sell-out, even with its increased print run of around 80 000. Copies were selling on eBay for $100 before the magazine was even off the newsstands. Princess Mary requested copies of the photographs to give as Christmas gifts. We continued to post the magazine to her every month, and when the couple's first son, Christian, was born in 2005, I went shopping for a gift. Envisaging a ballroom filled to the brim with presents, I nevertheless went to Adrienne & The Misses Bonney in Double Bay and chose an exquisite hand-stitched baby blanket, edged with rabbits wearing full-red satin skirts—red being the royal colour of Denmark. 'I had this blanket made with Princess Mary's baby in mind,' said the women at the sales desk, without me saying a word.

Several weeks later I received a handwritten note from the princess, thanking me. 'Little Christian loves pulling at the rabbit's skirts,' she wrote. The blanket had actually made it to the infant prince. The fairytale was complete.

11
SHOWTIME

Sitting front row at the international fashion shows is most certainly a glamorous aspect of an editor's job, but one that I always considered a privilege. For my first ten years at *Vogue*, ready-to-wear shows were not on the agenda for me, as they were reserved for the editor-in-chief and the fashion director only.

In the eighties and early nineties, for a country as small as Australia there were also very few invitations to go around, even for a *Vogue* title. Nancy Pilcher and Judith Cook had spent many seasons with a great deal of standing only tickets, and on occasions would even sneak into shows. That's what the fashion-obsessed did, and still do. Standing tickets were almost impossible to get for the really big shows, and the security at the door may decide at the last minute not to let you in at all. Most of the 'standing' was done outside, pleading with the *cravat rouge* (the doormen wearing red ties) to let you in. It's a kind of rite of passage when finally you get a ticket and there is a seat attached. If a label doesn't sell in your country, it's more than likely that you will only receive one ticket, or not be invited to the show at all.

The RTW shows are a business. If the house advertises in your magazine, you'll definitely have a seat. It may not be front row, but if you shoot enough editorial for them that season your seating allocation will gradually improve. The system of who, how many and where you will sit is forensically ruthless.

The RTW shows are held twice yearly: Spring/Summer in September and Autumn/Winter in March, and to attend all four—New York, London, Milan and Paris—means you are on the road for almost one month. For economic reasons we would attend Milan and Paris only, as coming from Australia it wasn't feasible for us to pop home for the weekend in between cities to see our families. It's a very expensive exercise, because a car and driver are required to negotiate the gruelling timetable—you may be seeing up to ten shows a day with showroom visits in between, in far-flung, traffic-choked locations all over each city. It's 9 a.m. starts, 11 p.m. dinners, for three weeks straight.

The Haute Couture season is much more civilised, and elegant: three to four days in January and July, but unfortunately we did not have the budgets to send anyone from Australia. Only a small number of fashion houses, such as Chanel and Dior, produce couture—exquisite handworked and custom-fitted collections for a smattering of wealthy private clients.

It wasn't until I lived in Paris that I was able to register with the Chambre Syndicale, on behalf of *Vogue Australia* and *Vogue Singapore*, for both couture and ready-to-wear. The Chambre Syndicale, or *Fédération Française de la Couture*, is the regulating body of the French fashion industry. It decides on the dates the shows are held, which designers are invited to show on the official calendar, and whether your publication is considered valid enough to be listed for invitations. But being registered does not automatically mean you will receive a seat—that is up to the house itself, and the PR department.

Singapore was a larger commercial market than Australia, thus I received more tickets and better seating at shows such as Yves Saint Laurent and Christian Dior, but back in the early nineties Asia wasn't especially front-of-mind for the French or Italian PRs. More than a few of them thought Asia was one big place, until you explained that China, Indonesia, Singapore, Malaysia, Thailand, and so on, were significantly different countries.

The Australian market hardly rated in the minds of the French either. Jean Paul Gaultier was one of the hottest tickets at the time, and his PR was one of the most difficult. Difficult is a relative term, but in his case it meant that you could never, ever get put through to him on the phone. If a fashion house does not intend to give you a seat, it's not going to happen, no matter how much you plead. It is impossible to change their minds. An intern will say 'The capacity of the show is very small this season', and hang up on you.

One afternoon, I asked Mourad to call the Gaultier office as I was desperate for an invitation to the upcoming show. When I was feeling fragile and Australian, I had poor Mourad do all the pleading. By some miracle he got through to the PR, presumably because he was French.

He went through the motions of asking for a ticket on my behalf and received a swift 'Non' in return.

'But it's *Vogue*,' Mourad protested, rather naively. '*Vogue Australia* is important isn't it?'

'No. Not at all,' came the brutally honest reply.

In the twenty-two months I spent at *Harper's Bazaar* as associate editor I attended the RTW shows on my own and received so few invitations I once called editor Karin Upton Baker from Paris and asked if I could come home. There is nothing more frustrating, lonely and wasteful than being on the circuit, acutely aware that you are missing out on important shows or private parties.

When I went to *Vogue Australia* as editor, one of our biggest challenges was to make sure we improved the standing of the magazine in terms of status and show access. The more insider information and experiences you are privy to, the better you are at your job. Take away the shows, the travel, the one-on-one opportunities to see things up close, then you can hardly call yourself an expert.

Australia is very far away from the epicentre of fashion. Yes, digital media has changed everything, and you can watch the Burberry show live-streamed from London, but to really be an authority on a subject you have to live and breathe it. Present the fashion on a hologram by all means, but I also want to look across the runway and see the real Kate Moss in the front row. My fashion editors and I slogged away at it every season, meeting and getting to know all the PRs, visiting every showroom, shooting the merchandise in the months following, interviewing the designers, sending them magazines and 'tear sheets' every month to let them know how much coverage we had given them. Gradually we increased the recognition and respect for the magazine to the point that we would always receive two tickets to every show, one of them generally being in the front row—two if we were lucky.

Most people would assume that because you're with *Vogue* a red carpet is rolled out of your limousine and a minion will arrive to show you to your chair next to Anna Wintour. Ah, no. You have to earn your seat on the bench. Circumstances and pecking orders have changed so much now though, there will probably be a really thin, beautiful, Russian trust fund-blogger wearing current season Balmain and an online retail buyer from Iceland in front of you anyway.

Shortly before the Princess Mary project, Gabriele resigned and I was left with the role of fashion director to fill. Naomi Smith was working at *Marie Claire*, and was my first choice to join the *Vogue* team given that she and I had trained together for so many years under the previous regimes of both June McCallum and Nancy Pilcher. I hired her, and Naomi and I subsequently shared a wonderful eight years of attending the shows together, twice a year, where we would be on the road for almost three weeks straight. On the odd occasion that only one of us could go, I would always nominate Naomi. Your fashion director has to see the shows. They have different antennae to an editor. While I obviously know a good show or a bad show when I see it, I probably tend to have a more 'big picture' approach, looking at the scene in an overall context of how we would capture the next fashion season trends, whereas Naomi could pinpoint the micro immediately. Upon leaving a show I would say, 'That was great', and she would respond, 'Yes, exit 11 was the best, and the shoe that came out on exit 4 is a must-have, and that new, young, blonde model from Belgium who looks like a boy is the one to watch', and she would be absolutely right about all of it.

Very often, by the time we'd made our request for the samples she had selected for photography, they would already be in the US *Vogue* stockroom because they were in fact the highlight pieces, and the model of the moment would be completely booked up by the big name magazines, and thus out of the question for us. Thank goodness there was often a second press rack of samples in Asia where we could send our requests.

The model situation was not so easy. This is where you had to make sure you had the model agency bookers on side. They could either give you a top Australian girl, a rising star, or, if you were really lucky, half a day with a big star, all with a cover demanded.

Another misconception, among the many, is that when you work at *Vogue* and want to book a model, you simply call the agency and they reply, 'Of course—*Vogue*,' and give you a date that works perfectly for everyone concerned. Not so. Model wrangling is one of the most time-consuming and exasperating components of the magazine business. All the elements of a shoot are inter-twined, politically. A big name international model will only work with a particular pool of photographers who are considered by their agency to be 'hot'. If you are Paris *Vogue*, no problem, but many of the 'hot' photographers were not interested in working for *Vogue Australia*, or were too costly for us to afford. Or the agency would suggest some new rising star photographer (probably a good-looking guy) who all the models loved, and demand we promise a cover, despite the fact that his body of work was mainly grimy, grainy and totally uncommercial.

Fortunately, many of the Australian models came to be a dominant force in the international fashion industry, major-league girls like

Abbey Lee Kershaw and Catherine McNeil, who loved being on the cover back home and were happy to shoot with our top local photographers, like Max Doyle and Nicole Bentley, whenever they were in town. It is a very complex and sometimes frustrating exercise to put the best teams together.

The negotiations we went through so we could feature a pregnant Miranda Kerr on what would be her very first cover for *Vogue Australia* are a case in point. I had lunch with Miranda and her agent at the Hôtel Costes in Paris, immediately after she had modelled in the highly sought-after Balenciaga show. She breezed through the hotel lobby, trying to avoid the paparazzi, and over grilled sole and green salad we discussed potential photographers. There was one international photographer Miranda was adamant she wanted us to hire, so Naomi and I duly contacted his agent and arranged to meet at Hôtel Le Meurice. When we arrived he was one of those condescending French agents who could barely disguise his disdain, but was secretly thinking his photographer should do the job because Miranda Kerr had become so influential.

It was about two weeks into the RTW shows and I was tired and cranky. The agent started blithering on about timings and costs and business-class flights and how famous his client was and what stylist he insisted on using, until I couldn't be bothered to humour him anymore. I didn't think the photographer was that talented anyway. 'Look,' I said. 'I've been doing this a long time. Don't patronise me. I know exactly where *Vogue Australia* sits in the scheme of things. But Miranda Kerr is requesting this, so why don't you work out whether you want it or not.' That stopped him. He then said, looking down his nose at me: 'Well, I think the only possible way we can do it is if she is completely naked in the whole shoot.' The last time I looked, *Vogue* was a fashion magazine, so we parted company.

Miranda did end up completing the shoot with us, with her preferred local photographer Carlotta Moye. And she even wore clothes.

Every show season also involved attending the *Vogue* dinner in Paris, which was hosted by Jonathan Newhouse. Invitees included all the international *Vogue* managing directors, editors and fashion directors (excepting the US, which is a separate company to Condé Nast International), and a smattering of top designers and photographers. It was a reasonably intimate group of around seventy-five, and always held in smallish, traditional fine dining restaurants—never anywhere overly trendy.

Those dinners were a daunting experience to say the least, especially from the sartorial angle. Could there be a tougher crowd to dress for? The first dinner I attended as editor I was placed next to Stella McCartney, and over the next thirteen years I would have the pleasure of meeting Riccardo Tisci, Rick Owens, Dries van Noten, Consuela Castiglioni from Marni, photographer Mario Testino, Roland Mouret, Gareth Pugh, Sarah Burton from Alexander McQueen, Peter Dundas, Peter Copping and Alber Elbaz.

One of my favorite people to be seated alongside was *Vogue Italia* fashion editor, the late Anna Piaggi, who was the sweetest person you could hope to meet and had a great affinity for Australia, as she had visited many times with her good friend, Melbourne-born fashion historian Vern Lambert.

I'm an outgoing person, and can certainly hold my own at a party, but the *Vogue* dinners were intimidating. Wrongly or not, I always felt somewhat inconsequential among the ranks of the bigger, more powerful *Vogues*, such as British, French and Italian. And if Carine Roitfeld, the glamorous and surprisingly friendly ex-editor-in-chief of Paris *Vogue* was in the room wearing current-season Pucci, forget it.

Each season, Naomi and I would stress out at the hotel beforehand, worrying about what to wear, and then console each other with the fact that no one would be looking at us anyway. Jonathan would always do the same speech and refer to us as one big Condé Nast family, but there were undoubtedly more favoured children. I took some comfort in noticing that many of the designers often appeared nervous themselves, but it was nothing a couple of shots of vodka and some caviar blinis couldn't help alleviate.

Despite the killer nerves it was always thrilling to be among the calibre of talent that Condé Nast attracted, even if you weren't exactly swapping mobile numbers. One hot, sticky afternoon in Milan, all the editors, including Anna Wintour, were invited to Giorgio Armani's private residence for afternoon tea. This was a highly unusual invitation and I arrived late and flushed, having been stuck in terrible traffic. As I dashed up the stairs and burst in the door, Jonathan Newhouse turned to me and said, 'Hello Kirstie, you know Mr Armani don't you?' It just so happened I was well acquainted with Mr Armani, so after he and I exchanged greetings Jonathan continued. 'And you know Anna (Wintour), and of course Roger Federer.' I had to wing it from there.

Despite all the glamorous extracurricular activities, the shows were always our main focus. These could be sometimes dull or ill-judged, but I always found them inspiring. There is so much to take in aside from the fashion; watching the world's top models in motion with the addition of music, lighting, hair and makeup is a joy. But many shows do still resonate, such as the Gucci ones when Tom Ford fever was at its peak and all you wanted was a seat with a vantage point where you could actually see the shoes. I will also never forget John Galliano for Dior in 2007 (I had a small tear at the Madame Butterfly couture show for its sheer mastery), Alexander McQueen (especially one evening presentation in the spooky shadows of the Concergerie in Paris accompanied by wolves pacing in their cages), any Chanel show, (because it's Chanel and Chanel is Paris), Louis Vuitton's fetishistic 'Night Porter'-inspired collection, Jil Sander's purism, Dolce & Gabbana's Italian sensuality, Dries van Noten's global mélange of references, Givenchy's edginess, Marni's kooky prettiness, Yves Saint Laurent's perfection and Prada's intellectualism.

There is also a level of style that surrounds showtime that intrinsically informs your understanding and taste level: the *aperitivo* before the Prada show and the glass it is served in, the amazing buffet lunch at the Tod's showroom, the canapés at the Roger Vivier boutique, the unbelievable food served at the Armani parties, are all a wondrous part of the fashion week experience. I remember being in the Sergio Rossi showroom on the Via Montenapoleone in Milan, admiring the coming season's shoes, drinking a blood orange cocktail and snacking on tiny morsels of various perfection, silently thanking the heavens and knowing: 'Yes, there are worse jobs.'

People watching was obviously another bonus of the shows, especially coming from a country that is, shall we say, somewhat stylistically challenged.

In the early days I enjoyed seeing what other members of the fashion press were wearing, not to mention all the buyers, socialites, top customers and celebrities. But it was certainly not the circus it has become today. Photographers were there to shoot the runway fashion and the celebrities, and perhaps some of the select media. But since the emergence of the street-style photographer and blogger, the amount of 'poseurs' that exist outside and inside the shows has become a whole new business. The coverage of street fashionistas of indeterminate means is as important as the designer content, and may even be devoted more space. With e-tail click-through-and-buy options attached to the live streaming of a show, the consumer entered the conversation, one that was only previously afforded to privileged critics. Social media has democratised fashion commentary and created a new order of power players in the industry. Decades of experience at revered mastheads and the ability to articulate intelligently may prove to be of very little value in the near future. There are now show attendees who are sponsored to wear and promote a particular fashion house—a walking product placement. This had always been the domain of celebrities but with the arrival of new media it has shifted to civilians.

It's getting harder to find honest, relevant criticism because the new fashion commentators are relentlessly positive in their reviews. It's within their interest to be so. They want to go to the shows. I would like to see more of them be truly critical, especially if they are in the fortunate position of not yet having any advertisers who could pull out. I couldn't manage to get to the coffee being served at the Max Mara show last season because a blogger was blocking the way, taking an Instagram of the croissants. I did wonder then: 'At what point do we have saturation coverage?' I have increasingly thought that there are too many very smart people in the world writing overblown nonsense about fashion.

* * *

There was also, of course, Australian Fashion Week (AFW) in Sydney every May, our own antipodean version of the RTW circuit, cleverly designed and strategised in 1995 by Simon Lock, a savvy marketer and entrepreneur.

Simon did a magnificent job of galvanising a very opinionated and initially naive industry to put on a first-class fashion week. There have been some truly wonderful moments at AFW, including Akira Isogawa debuting his collection in the very first year in a group show—with the models wearing red socks because that was all he could afford. Collette Dinnigan also put on numerous beautiful, high quality presentations and dinners that were generous and polished, while the New Zealanders such as Karen Walker, Kate Sylvester and Zambesi always added a quiet intelligence.

Michelle Jank wowed the audience with her lovely jewel-encrusted capsule collection that was snapped up by Brown's in the UK. Easton Pearson, Sass & Bide, Zimmermann, Therese Rawsthorne and Josh Goot collections continually shone. Peter Morrissey's shows were standing room only and had a sexy Aussie party vibe that was contagious and glamorous. Renegade collective Ksubi created global headlines when they sent hordes of rats down a clear Perspex runway, which certainly achieved what they were after: a great deal of front-row squirming—me in particular, as I can't bear rodents. I don't remember the clothes whatsoever but I appreciated the insolence of it. I also always loved the Romance Was Born shows which were crazy, inspired, original and completely uncommercial, which I believe should be allowed of a young designer for a period of time, until the harsh reality of business sets more practical constraints. The Dion Lee introductory show held in an underground carpark was perhaps the most accomplished first entrance ever seen at AFW, in so far as its maturity and precision went, and Christopher Esber's original and masterly collection in 2012 could have been on a Paris runway. In among a lot of hype, and a little amateurism, there were always some gems.

It was interesting to return to Sydney after the RTW shows and plunge into AFW just six weeks afterwards, because you couldn't help making comparisons to what you had just seen overseas—especially if a local collection was obviously derivative, which was unfortunately quite common. I missed the very first AFW as I was still in Paris, but I was part of Marion Hume's *Vogue* team for the second and I remember being surprised at the backlash she received when she levelled some blunt advice towards the Australian designers. She had praise for many, and was a big champion of Collette Dinnigan and Akira Isogawa, among others, but it seemed that an informed opinion from a seasoned international journalist was unwelcome. Australian designers are unused to criticism and many of them expect a level of editorial praise that outweighs their talent. I'm of the belief that AFW's founder Simon Lock deserves a medal and/or the Order of Australia for the egotistical crap he had to endure over the years from certain designers. And a sometimes surprisingly hostile black-and-white press, with an agenda, it seemed, to wipe Fashion Week off the map because we were all a pack of wankers.

In the pre-online era, the rivals to magazines were the newspaper supplements, so we took them on and produced our own mini supplements to cover Fashion Week. We had to work until late into the night to shoot and turn around a supplement in five days and attach it to the next issue.

For the third year of AFW I was at *Bazaar* and we slaved until the early hours all week to get the supplement to the printers—this at the end of long, long days seeing shows. Back then we were dealing with film, not digital images, so the editing process was excruciating. It was all hands on deck. After the issue had gone on sale I received a phone call from a leading designer. His show hadn't been all that great. In fact, it was also a shameless rip-off, and the clothes were badly made. But we had very generously shot an entire head-to-toe look in the main-page fashion 'well' (the section of the magazine with no ads), and had run a review and several runway images in the trends pages. He wasn't an advertiser. For some crazy reason, when I picked up the phone I thought he was going to thank me, but he had called to complain because, in our exhausted haste, it transpired that one of the runway shots had been mistakenly captioned. I decided then and there, that in future, if a designer's collection wasn't up to standard, they weren't going to get any coverage. There was no good reason for the charade to continue, because the one losing out was the reader.

As AFW continued, the coverage moved away from those gruelling nights at the office producing a print product, to online reviewing. When News Limited took over the license for Condé Nast, I convinced the then CEO Tony Kendall to appoint crack journalist Damien Woolnough as the editor of *vogue.com.au* in 2008, and his acerbic coverage increased traffic to the website exponentially. Immediacy had become the new currency. No one was going to wait a month for the magazine's verdict. Our mandate was an informed viewpoint and that was clear in our online edit. If a show was good, it got reviewed. Ordinary, and the shots were posted, unreviewed. Bad, and it didn't appear at all.

In a very short space of time, technology had completely shifted how information was translated from the runway to the consumer, and it continues to evolve. Experiencing a show virtually through your handheld device is one thing. But there's nothing quite like being front row in Milan chatting to Tim Blanks.

12
SOCIAL STUDIES

Shortly after the 2000 Olympics in Sydney, the managing director of Giorgio Armani in Australia, Mary Chiew, extended a grand invitation to me. Would I like to travel to New York to attend the gala opening of the Armani retrospective to be held at the Guggenheim? Oh, and by the way, Ian Thorpe would be joining us.

I have no interest in sport whatsoever, but even I am not un-Australian enough to ignore the swimming. Ian had just won three gold and two silver medals at the Olympics. He was a national hero.

I was beside myself with excitement over the idea of meeting him, and so soon after his incredible achievements. I had arrived in New York and was in my hotel room dressing for dinner when Mary called and said: 'Come down to the bar and meet Ian and we'll go to dinner.' I was flustered the entire way down in the lift, which is highly unusual for me. He was so sweet and easygoing, and very assured for someone so young. We all set out for dinner at Nobu, and as I sat in the back of the town-car next to Ian, I glanced down and thought: 'There's those famous size 17 feet.'

I began asking him some searingly intelligent questions along the lines of, 'Gee, what do you think about when you're doing all those laps?' but Ian was patient with his responses. We ordered sushi, which he had never tasted before, so I was a tiny bit thrilled that I was there with the Thorpedo when he tried raw fish for the first time. There was a famous actress in the restaurant—I don't recall who—and I, like an idiot reminded Ian that he was going to be famous forever in Australia. Forever. For the rest of his life. I made a big point of driving it home. He stared at me with a slightly horrified look on his face and said: 'Thanks for that thought Kirstie. I just turned eighteen.'

The following night was the star-studded opening of the spectacular Giorgio Armani retrospective, filled with the likes of Jeremy Irons, Destiny's Child, Patti Smith and Robert de Niro. During the evening I wandered alone into a room where the famous scene from the film *American Gigolo* was screening, the one where a handsome, shirtless Richard Gere proceeds to lay out his Armani clothes on the bed, choosing a tie for each shirt. At that very moment, a handsome, clothed Richard Gere walked in, saw me watching the younger him on the video, and grinned. I nearly died. His wife, the stunning actress Carey Lowell, made an entrance shortly afterwards, and I was equally thrilled to be in her presence. I adore *Law & Order*. Another *Law & Order* alumni Angie Harmon was there too, one of the most gorgeous women I've ever seen. They made my night.

The following evening Ian and I attended the VH1 Fashion Awards, a sort of celebration of fashion and music with no earthly purpose, which was also packed wall-to-wall with celebrities from fashion, music and film. I lost Ian on the red carpet because by this stage all the paparazzi knew who he was and were calling out 'Thorpedo, Thorpedo!' so I happily made my own way down, trying not to look plain and incongruous. There were reporters stopping all the stars; one crew who kept repeating, 'We're from an internet channel, do you use the internet?' It seems so prehistoric now, but a great deal of the celebrities replied no, they didn't have time. Supermodel Gisele Bündchen said not really, but she used email.

I was drinking in all the glamour when I was suddenly dazzled from either side. The queue had stalled and I found myself wedged between Beyoncé in front, Jennifer Lopez behind. They have to be two of the most beautiful women on the planet, with the most perfect bottoms. I've met hundreds—no, thousands—of the world's best looking people, but Beyoncé and J. Lo are beyond words. They literally glow. Now I really did look plain and incongruous.

Once we were inside the auditorium and seated the evening turned hilarious for many reasons—not just because the awards were so random and pointless—but we also discovered that actor Ben Stiller was in the house, filming a scene for his upcoming film *Zoolander*. We were told that it required audience participation: when musician Lenny Kravitz announced that the Male Model of the Year was 'Hansel', Stiller, playing the part of the character Derek Zoolander, was going to rush up on stage to claim the award and we were to pretend to be shocked and embarrassed for him. As it happened I was seated two rows behind Ben Stiller, so in the film I am a blur in the frame when he leaps from his chair.

We had to run through the performance twice, and everyone in the crowd overacted madly. I have such a soft spot for that film.

It's one of the most astute movies about fashion ever made. What really happens in the fashion world is sometimes so ridiculous, it requires a Zoolander level of irony to even come close to replicating it. I am quite proud to be able to claim I'm an extra in *Zoolander*.

Ian and I went to the afterparty, and as I pushed through the crush and stepped up to the bar the gentleman next to me moved graciously out of my way to allow me to order first. It was Sir Paul McCartney. The barman almost fainted with delight when he saw him. I lost Ian again. I think Jennifer Lopez asked him to join her table.

It certainly was a brilliant night.

* * *

It was again thanks to the incomparable Mr Armani that in 2006 I was offered another once in a lifetime opportunity, this time to join him and a very small group of journalists on a tour of Hong Kong and Shanghai.

The day of my arrival in Hong Kong I was taken to meet Mr Armani, who was doing a walk-through of the enormous Armani shopping complex in Chater House, checking on the refurbishment of the Armani bar and the Armani Casa interiors store. My lovely friend Sally Pitt (head of Armani PR in Sydney), and I picked our way gingerly through the construction site and she introduced me to Mr Armani, who was surveying the scene, impeccable in his navy pants and sweater and bright-white sneakers. 'This is the editor of *Vogue Australia*,' said Sally. 'And what a beautiful editor!' he exclaimed in Italian, kissing me on both cheeks. I'm sure he says that to all the editors but it worked and I immediately developed a crush on him.

There were only a handful of journalists on the trip, which meant that we had incredible proximity to Mr Armani throughout the entire six days. It was as if we were on tour with him.

The first evening in Hong Kong we were treated to an Armani Privé show, which is the couture arm of his collections. Mr Armani does not speak English, but will speak in French, so when the PR discovered I could hold my own in that language I was placed next to him for most lunches and dinners. It was such an honour to spend time with this great designer, there in the inner sanctum of Armani. Also on the trip was his niece Roberta, who was an absolute delight. She and I bonded over lunch at the Cipriani in Hong Kong when I asked her what she had wanted to do before she joined the family firm and she replied: 'Acting.' Given that I am Australian, we moved on to the obvious. 'I love Russell Crowe!' exclaimed Roberta to which I protested, 'No, I love him more!' and we spent a good half an hour raving about Russell and *Gladiator* and Maximus and how we could dream up an event in Sydney to which we would invite him so we could sit either side. Roberta, of course, had actually already met Russell in Rome after *Gladiator* was released, and shared a car with him, which had driven around the exterior of the Coliseum.

The Armani team were so inclusive and so effortlessly chic in their navy-blue cardigans and trainers, I wanted to join the family. I even flew with Mr Armani from Hong Kong to Shanghai, and it was remarkable to see the stir he causes when he is out in public. He is as striking as he is famous, with his white hair gleaming against his tanned face. For the flight, he wore a white t-shirt under his navy jacket that said A1. 'It's always my seat number,' he laughed. I complimented him on the scent he was wearing and he sweetly gave me the bottle, which was a lab sample that the fragrance house was working on. I still have it.

When we arrived at Shanghai airport, the 72-year-old Mr Armani, true gentleman that he is, walked over to the baggage carousel and picked up my suitcase.

There were many more dinners and lunches in Shanghai, one I recall that had about ten courses of food, every one of them a greenish black colour. Mr Armani skipped that one, as he much preferred to eat Italian, traditional-style: three courses, one glass of wine. He is so disciplined and energetic, I found him to be a real inspiration. I spoke at length to him throughout the tour, culminating in an interview conducted on a sunny outdoor terrace after lunch. He had me hooked: on his values, his taste, his remarkable work ethic. By the end of the week I was tossing up buying a navy Emporio Armani outfit and some sneakers and just following them all back to Milan, hoping they wouldn't notice I hadn't gone home. By that time, I was even of the belief that I spoke Italian.

At another memorable dinner in Shanghai on the same trip, I was seated next to the Chinese actress Zhang Ziyi, of *Crouching Tiger, Hidden Dragon* fame (who told me, of all things, that she was looking for a boyfriend), and Armani's royal ambassador, Lady Helen Taylor. The restaurant was abuzz that Mr Armani was in the room. We were then joined by a very dashing Arab sheik. Mr Armani effortlessly pulls the world's most rich and famous into his orbit, every minute of the day, and I was so utterly privileged to have been included. While it was an obvious expectation that there would be coverage of my trip in the magazine, such unparalleled access equalled a more profound understanding of the designer and the brand. It's the elegant and intelligent way to do things.

He visited Sydney the following year, in 2007, to attend a dinner at the Sydney Theatre Company and be acknowledged as a patron by the STC artistic directors Cate Blanchett and her husband Andrew Upton. I joined up with the Armani posse once again, and we all ended up at Trademark nightclub in Kings Cross, Roberta and I chatting on a banquette while Mr Armani promptly got mobbed. Not quite the same level as the China experience.

In May 2010 I returned to Shanghai, this time to attend a Dior Cruise show and the lavish afterparty. The day of the show I was granted a very quick meeting and interview with designer John Galliano, on the vertiginous 93rd floor of the Park Hyatt hotel. I had never met Galliano, despite many seasons spent admiring his dazzling couture and RTW shows. On this occasion he was accompanied by a number of PRs who stayed in the room while we chatted, which I always find terribly disconcerting. I think it's impossible to conduct a thorough and spontaneous interview when there is a PR present constantly looking at their watch.

Galliano wore his hair in braids, a jaunty feather in his hat, rolled-up trousers and a vest. I was taken aback by how handsome he was, with golden skin and huge brown eyes. He was so guileless and unaffected, sitting close to me on the lounge and flicking through an album, showing me photographs from his recent travels. He was chain-smoking cigarettes which he lit with a huge crocodile-Dunhill table lighter, and drinking a juice at the same time. 'Detox, re-tox,' he joked.

A model entered wearing one of the exits we would be seeing that night, and he took me piece by piece through the 'Nouvelle Vague' collection which was hanging on a rack nearby. I cannot say that we had a particularly profound conversation, but I found him to be charming. I watched with sadness as the unfortunate events at Dior later unfolded, and he was dismissed due to anti-Semitic remarks. Galliano was such a global traveller in real life and in his wondrous collections, the incident seems so incongruous. I do hope he returns to the world of fashion one day. I'd love to interview him again—with no one else in the room.

There were many other trips around the world, quaffing champagne at fabulous parties courtesy of the great fashion houses, in particular the incomparable Louis Vuitton. In 2000 I found myself chatting to Xena, Warrior Princess, aka actress Lucy Lawless, at an ice bar in a ships dock in Auckland Harbour for the Louis Vuitton Cup. Another time, I was at a roller disco held in a spaceship that had been built in a Tokyo park, watching Grace Jones perform while the designer Marc Jacobs danced happily next to me. At perhaps the best party I have ever attended, I wandered through a mind-bending maze of curiosities in a London warehouse with Gwyneth Paltrow and Kirsten Dunst, and then clapped along to Donna Summer and Marc Jacobs singing together on stage.

No one puts on a party quite like Vuitton. For their new store opening in Rome in early 2012, the theme of the event was 'the world's oldest profession', and guests were propositioned by a cast of skilful actors who handed us bags of gold coins to 'pay' for services, all above-board and in good fun. I was chatting with Cate Blanchett at the event when we were asked to choose a 'partner' who was to take you into a room and recite some sort of soliloquy. I declined, and I'm not sure if Cate went through with it.

The following evening, the lucky journalists on the trip were treated to an evening visit to the Vatican and a private tour of the Sistine Chapel. After almost an hour in the chapel listening to the most wonderful guide explaining every detail, we were led outside to a magnificent corridor where trestle tables had been set up, with white-jacketed waiters serving Prosecco. In the Vatican. As you do.

Another trip to Tokyo, courtesy of the executive vice president of Global Communications for Calvin Klein, Malcolm Carfrae, who is an Aussie expatriate and a great friend. Over a long lunch at the Park Hyatt I interviewed both Francisco Costa, the designer of Calvin Klein Collection, and Kevin Carrigan, global creative director of ck Calvin Klein, who are both so talented, open and unpretentious. Although I was part of a group of Asia-Pacific journalists, the boys decided that I needed to stay with the Calvin Klein team and thus I ended up after the event at the official Calvin Klein company dinner, sitting in between Malcolm and Francisco. The company's CEO Tom Murry rose to congratulate everyone and talk a little business when he noticed me. 'Kirstie, you just need to put your hands over your ears for a few minutes,' he said.

Later that evening we ended up in a windowless, smoke-filled nightclub in Tokyo that was about the size of a small living room with the entire Calvin Klein team, and all the male models who had been part of the installation. Having the good fortune to be the only woman in the room, I began talking to one gorgeous nineteen-year-old boy from Germany, with the regulation floppy hair, long Roman nose and bee-stung lips. There was a line of them along the banquette who all looked exactly the same—that is, perfect. I started in with some unwanted lecture about how he should think about a career outside of modelling and once you'd done Calvin Klein you'd pretty much peaked, blah blah blah. He listened to me very politely until I stopped to take a self-important breath and said very politely, 'Thanks for your feedback. I should be okay. I'm studying to be a nuclear physicist.'

It is difficult to compare and contrast all the wondrous events that I was invited to be a part of, but the fortieth anniversary celebration of Ralph Lauren in New York would have to be a standout. My publisher Grant Pearce and I travelled together to attend the Spring 2008 collection show, as well as the black tie dinner afterwards for a select 450 people worldwide. The show was held in an enormous white tent that had been erected on the edge of Manhattan's Central Park Conservatory Garden. Immaculately dressed celebrities and guests filed past the enormous flower-filled urns at the park gates; they included Mayor Bloomberg, Robert F Kennedy Jr, Lauren Bush, Robert De Niro, Diane Sawyer, Dustin Hoffman, Donna Karan, Diane von Furstenberg, Barry Diller and Caroline Herrera. It was the pinnacle of American power, glamour and refinement.

The show itself was a triumph, and at the finale Ralph Lauren walked out to crazy applause and Frank Sinatra singing 'The Best is Yet to Come'. At that point the painted backdrop at the end of the runway slid back to reveal—with precision timing, and to great dramatic effect—a magical garden, replete with a flowing fountain, waiters with silver trays of champagne and a platform built high in the treetops strung with crystal chandeliers. This was where we would be dining.

Grant was so overcome by the perfection of it all, he burst into tears. I stood by the fountain and smiled at Barbara Walters, like it was the most normal thing in the world. As we mounted the stairs to our dinner in the sky, I chatted to Sarah Jessica Parker. I was seated beside an editor from the *Wall Street Journal* and we discussed the fact that Rupert Murdoch had just bought the newspaper, before Mayor Bloomberg began his toast to Ralph.

It so happened that I had struck up an acquaintance with Lauren Bush when she had been living and studying in Sydney, so she and I greeted each other and I met her soon-to-be husband, David Lauren, Ralph's son. Just like my previous daydreams in Denmark, I simply surrendered myself to the elegance and theatre of it all. I caught up with fellow editor-in-chief Christiane Arp from *Vogue Germany* a few days later and we both raved about the night. 'That's the sort of party that people think *Vogue* editors go to all the time,' she commented. She and I both agreed it was one of the most remarkable events we had ever witnessed. That night I had certainly seen the best of New York. Top of the heap.

* * *

In 2004, just prior to the Olympics, I flew to Athens with a photographic team to produce a Greek-inspired December issue featuring models Gemma Ward and Nicole Trunfio. While I was there, suffering through what proved to be the shoot from hell due to horribly dysfunctional team dynamics, I received an invitation from the editor-in-chief of *Vogue Greece*, Elena Makris, to attend a charity dinner she was hosting. The evening was to begin with a Luciano Pavarotti concert held in the ancient Odeon of Herodes Atticus Amphitheatre, followed by a glittering outdoor dinner on the slopes of the Acropolis.

My great friend, the hugely successful makeup guru Napoleon Perdis, was also on the trip—thank goodness—and was thrilled for me to have the chance to experience the country of his heritage in such a profoundly glamorous way. I went to his suite at the sumptuous Hotel Grande Bretagne in Syntagma Square before the evening's proceedings, and he generously did my makeup, as he has done on numerous occasions. I adore makeup and I adore Napoleon, so we're a good pair. It's a tough call to say who loves eyeliner more.

The Pavarotti concert was of course sublime, especially in the historic and ambient amphitheatre. As I made my way to dinner afterwards I was touched to find that Elena had placed me at one of the head tables and I was seated next to supermodel Naomi Campbell, and opposite legendary British photographer David Bailey. Naomi was wearing a pleated Grecian-goddess silk dress and had delicate braids through her hair, also Grecian-style. She was shimmering. She is a spectacular beauty. Naomi has a reputation for being tricky, but I found her to have a charm that was completely disarming. She had recently been to New Zealand, and we chatted over dinner about the Maori culture, and life in general. David Bailey was also friendly and witty, with a soft spot for Australia, as he had once made a photographic trip around the outback solo. On a balmy night in Athens, with the illuminated ruins of the Acropolis behind us and a star-filled sky overhead, I did remind myself, yet again, what a privilege it was to work for *Vogue*.

That was until I got stuck in the middle of the Plaka by myself at 2 a.m., because my budget didn't stretch to a hire car.

13

AIRBRUSHES WITH FAME

We continued the tradition we started with Karl Lagerfeld's guest editorship of the December 2003 issue and kept exploring subjects we could feature for special editions. Crown Princess Mary featured on the December 2004 cover, and in 2005 we celebrated the success of Australian model Gemma Ward with a guest-edited issue. Come late 2006, my next guest editor wish was Kylie Minogue.

Kylie had been dealing with breast cancer and was just coming out the other side. Once the news was made public that she was in recovery, I made contact with her management about a possible collaboration. The answer at first was no, and I accepted that it may have been too soon to ask, but shortly afterwards I received an email advising me that they would like to go ahead with the project.

This was another interview that I was very keen to conduct myself. I had enormous admiration for the way she had managed her illness and even more so for the fact that she was prepared to talk to *Vogue* at this stage. I wasn't sure how well she was, and how much she could contribute, but I decided we could work around it, and what she was unable to deliver we would.

Our interview took place at Blakes Hotel in Kensington, London. I checked in the night before and awoke to the sound of creaking floorboards and the shuffling of feet in the early hours of the morning, as if a ghost was pottering around the room. The following day I had an appointment with Jacqui, aka Lady Lilac, a renowned psychic who had been recommended to me by a friend. It's a hobby of mine, harmless I hope. I'm counting on my friends to pull me aside if I start to get obsessive. (Mind you, I did find myself with my good friend Shemi visiting a toothless Bosnian gypsy in a field in Montenegro not so long ago, while mangy chickens ran around our feet, so maybe it's already too late.)

As Jacqui walked into my suite the telephone rang, but when I picked it up there was no one on the line. She glanced around and said: 'Someone was in here last night.' She then sat down, pulled out the tarot cards and before she even shuffled said: 'You're going to write a book, about yourself.'

I replied: 'No, I have no intention of writing a book about myself.'

I must send her a copy.

That afternoon I met with Kylie in the restaurant downstairs at Blakes, which is dark, cosy and dimly lit—very much like a chic opium den. I arrived at the appointed time, suddenly and unannounced, to find her curled up on a banquette speaking quietly to then boyfriend Olivier Martinez. I apologised for interrupting what looked to be a very private conversation, but they were both very courteous and Olivier made a quick exit. We ordered tea, and I broke the ice by handing Kylie two gifts, one a pearl bracelet from Paspaley, and the other, a handbag from Anya Hindmarsh. We very rarely came bearing gifts for celebrities, and the magazine certainly did not fund such a practice, but many companies like to have a star experience—and hopefully promote—their products. This was not the case in this instance; they were simply given out of goodwill.

I have to admit I was floored by how genuinely excited and grateful she was. I have seen a spoilt brat American actress literally throw a ring she had just been gifted on the floor of her hotel room. Kylie explained that this sort of largesse did not exist when she first started out and it reminded me just how long and how hard she has worked at her career. She was honest, thoughtful and professional during the interview and it remains one of my favourites. That a major star like Kylie—who was quite frankly a perfect stranger—would share such intimate details of her personal life with me was rather humbling.

One stipulation of our deal was that she would be photographed by her friend and stylist William Baker, a condition that, if we did not agree to it, was a deal breaker. Kylie's great friends Dolce & Gabbana provided the fashion from the current collection which Naomi Smith styled in a studio in London, and although Baker worked diligently, he was inexperienced and it showed in the photographs. Kylie still seemed frail, and his lighting hardened her, which was a shame. However, she was a trooper in every respect and did a beautiful personal photo diary for the magazine, featuring, without us asking, the bracelet and the bag. She is a superstar, inside and out.

Australian actresses have always been essential to *Vogue* and rarely have we experienced attitude. Quite the opposite. Rose Byrne has graced the cover many times, but I recall one time when she came from London to meet Naomi and I at our not particularly flash hotel in Paris. With no first-class airfare demands, she had paid for her own Eurostar ticket and checked in with no fanfare. I telephoned her room and asked if she would like to join us for dinner, as I had reserved a table at Hôtel Costes. 'Oh, I'd love to,' she said. On the way in a taxi, she asked me if I wouldn't mind stopping at an automatic teller machine. 'Do you need cash?' I asked. 'Yes,' she replied. 'So I can pay for my dinner.'

Another one of our favourites was the drop-dead gorgeous Melissa George, who Richard Bailey captured in a beautiful shoot at Napoleon's private home in the Hollywood hills. She is so generous she would quite literally give you the clothes off her back. Once we were dining at Icebergs in Bondi and she had just stepped off a plane from Los Angeles, looking like a genuine old-school movie star in head-to-toe Calvin Klein. I commented on how much I liked her cat-eye Oliver Peoples sunglasses and she said, 'Here, have them,' and insisted I keep them. She tried to do the same thing on another instance with a Calvin Klein evening bag, but I fought her off. She has become a good friend, but I've stopped complimenting her on things in case she tries to give them to me.

* * *

By the end of 2006, rumours started to circulate that the FPC magazine group was up for sale, and that Rupert Murdoch's News Limited was the main contender to buy it. Early one morning, a panicky message from management was sent around the building to say that Rupert himself was coming in, and telling us to start cleaning up. I privately questioned the rationale behind rushing to tidy the art department. I was pretty sure Rupert was used to the normal creative jumble of a working magazine office.

I was at my desk chatting to Tory Collison when a group of agitated suits burst through the door, circling Rupert. The only unflustered one was News Limited CEO John Hartigan, whom I'd never met. I was introduced to Rupert, and after we exchanged pleasantries I walked them all down to the fashion area, for the lack of anything more productive to do. Rupert was extremely relaxed, while the hovering FPC executives appeared to be on the brink of nervous collapse. There was a slightly awkward silence until John Hartigan stepped in, looked squarely at me and said, 'You know, Condé Nast hold you in very high regard indeed Kirstie,' in earshot of all. It probably wasn't true, but it was a lovely thing to say. He's a class act.

The News Limited deal was sealed in 2007 and for a short while we were unsure of who our new boss would be. But during a discussion with John Hartigan in his office at Holt Street, I learned that Michael McHugh was on his way out, and later it was announced he was being replaced by Tony Kendall, director of sales at News Limited.

Tony was, put simply, a nice guy: smart, fun and open to listening to what Grant and I had to say about our side of the business. In addition, he believed in print. The new chief operating officer was Sandra Hook, who had previously been the group publishing director at FPC and was also honest, intelligent and tactical. The future seemed very promising, given the combined clout of News Limited and the power of the *Vogue* brand.

Shortly after Tony started, the Condé Nast International conference rolled around, again in Venice. Nancy, Tony and I attended and he blended in easily, even volunteering to present one of the workshops—a task I would have dived into the murky depths of the canals to avoid. During the conference, Jonathan Newhouse, chairman of Condé Nast International, came over to me and remarked, 'I like your new CEO. He's really Australian, but in a good way.' That compliment is the highest praise an Australian will ever hope to get from Condé Nast, so well done to Tony Kendall.

News Limited were equally as inclusive of me (at the beginning), and I was later invited to join an executive conference in Canberra, being one of only a handful of women in the room. I thoroughly enjoyed those conferences, as it was real inner workings of the newspaper, corridors of power stuff that I found to be quite exhilarating. Their world was new to me, as I had never experienced such a male-dominated organisation. I could not help but feel the elitist nature of *Vogue* was at odds somewhat with News Limited's unashamedly anti-elitist philosophy. I overdressed just for the hell of it.

One evening during that first conference we assembled for drinks at Parliament House, as it was just prior to the 2007 federal election and John Hartigan told me they liked to stir things up. Both the government and opposition leaders were in attendance and I spoke with several politicians, including prime-ministers-to-be Kevin Rudd and Julia Gillard, until the then prime minister John Howard brushed past me on his way out, did a small double take, and introduced himself. Maybe because he'd never seen a News Limited journalist wearing head-to-toe Lanvin at one of these events.

Shortly afterwards I was invited to a dinner at est. restaurant. Only the major newspaper editors from around the country, some top management, me and Karen McCartney from *Inside Out* magazine, were on the guest list. I had apparently neglected to read the cc line of the email, because when I arrived at the bar Karen relayed to me that

Rupert Murdoch would also be attending. Thus I found myself in the private dining room with a dozen or so top News Limited executives, seated next to John Hartigan and directly opposite Rupert, on the Thursday evening before the general election. This was a thrilling, hair-at-the-back-of-your-neck-standing-up experience for me. For once in my life I was quiet as I observed how everyone behaved around the 'boss', as John called him. The men managed to be blokey and deferential at the same time.

Rupert was loquacious and engaging, and held the floor for most of the night, but it quickly became clear no one was ever really going to challenge him on anything, opinion or fact, whether he was talking about Hillary Clinton or the Taliban. The fire alarm went off at one point, but it didn't deter Rupert from his monologue. I was waiting for the 'Now let me tell you what editorial you are to run regarding Howard and the election' *Citizen Kane*-type speech but it didn't happen, much to my disappointment. The general consensus around the table was that Australia was ready for a Labor government and as it transpired the following weekend, we were. I will always appreciate that Tony Kendall and John Hartigan included me at that dinner, as it was a rare glimpse into another, very fascinating media world.

Tony left *Vogue* and returned to News Limited a year or so later to be replaced as CEO at News Magazines by Sandra Hook. Over the next four years there would be a constant shifting of staff, especially of the old guard at *Vogue*. My beloved Grant Pearce moved to Hong Kong to work for Condé Nast Asia Pacific, the syndication office was shut down which meant the departure of editorial business manager Georgette Johnson, and Nancy also left the office to concentrate solely on *Vogue* in Asia. I was left to deal with a myriad of new and old News Limited staffers and consultants who, one after the other, offered me their unsubstantiated advice on how to run *Vogue*. Everyone had an opinion, on everything, from which font we should use to how features should never contain a whole page of copy only. God forbid the *Vogue* reader be faced with lots of words. I had an advertising sales manager tell me with a completely straight face that she didn't think the consumer would notice if we chopped sixteen pages of editorial out of each issue. Even if it was a 100-page edition.

During this time I was invited to have lunch with the principal designer for Barbie Collector, Robert Best, who was in Sydney from the US and planning some upcoming Australian launches for Barbie. I arrived at Icebergs restaurant straight from a portrait shoot of myself, and I was very dressed up, in a sort of fifties, B-grade actress mode, with false eyelashes, backcombed hair and a leopard-print chiffon shirt—high camp when I think about it. Robert and I got on like a house on fire. No one else could get a word in. I went into a reverie about what sort of Barbie I would like to see, a Tennessee Williams collection of ageing, broken Barbies based on *The Roman Spring of Mrs Stone* (she would come with house keys to be thrown down to dangerous strangers from her balcony), or a 'Blanche DuBois Barbie', with silk shawls to toss over light bulbs. We discussed the possibility of 'the mother from *The Bad Seed* Barbie', with a murderous little Rhoda included in the same pack. We had the most hysterical lunch, and I left buoyed by the thought that Barbie was in safe hands with someone as clever and post-modern ironic as Robert.

Some months later, I was at a party at Tracy Baker's, who was in charge of press and marketing for Robert's Australian events. Robert was back in Sydney and the guest of honour of the night. During the evening Robert came to me and said, 'I would like to present you with something as a token of our new friendship,' and passed me a black gift box. I lifted the lid and found the most beautiful illustration of me, portrayed as a Barbie, highly stylised and flattering, and dedicated to 'a living doll …' I thought that was it, and was so touched. Robert then said: 'No, no, look under the tissue.'

There was a doll. A Kirstie Clements Barbie. She had far thicker hair and a much smaller waist than me but she was wearing the same leopard-print and black outfit that I had been wearing at our initial lunch and she had my eye makeup. I really did not know what to think or feel. Me, a Barbie? My friend Ian Clark, who was with me, was completely overcome. Everybody had tears in their eyes. I am the only Australian ever to be a Barbie. She/I even came with my own set of Chanel-style clothes and accessories, as well as a divine crocodile handbag.

It felt so weird, I put her/me straight back in the box and hid the doll behind the refrigerator for the rest of the night. I didn't like the thought of anyone touching her/me. As it turns out, I'm a collectors' item.

14

NEXT TOP DRAMA

In 2007, my publisher Grant Pearce came to me to discuss the opportunity for *Vogue* to get involved with the television series *Australia's Next Top Model* Season 3. The show, while it hadn't exactly produced a legitimate next top model, was by all accounts gaining popularity with viewers. To have a high fashion title such as *Vogue* involved would raise the stakes and credibility for both parties.

I had not seen the first two series, although my friend Napoleon Perdis had been involved and was a fan. Grant and I agreed that it would be good marketing for *Vogue*, as it would extend our reach into a new and different audience. Our part of the deal was that the winner would receive an eight-page fashion shoot in the magazine. Apart from a few appearances on various current affairs programmes I had little television experience, so I was slightly nervous, if only for reasons of vanity. I loathe being photographed; I'm almost phobic about it. Being thin and photogenic certainly would have made my public life easier.

The first *Vogue* segment was filmed at our offices, where I had a rack full of international designer labels to present to the contestants and quiz them on afterwards. The producers had prepared the questions beforehand, which were as basic as: 'Now who did I say was the designer of this dress, girls?' Of course any exercise on the show is completely irrelevant to the real world of modelling. Models don't need to know anything about anything. They don't even need to speak. They just need to be beautiful and show up on time.

In a different segment I had to rate them on their own personal style which felt slightly nasty, but that was the spin the show wanted. I was to appraise what they were wearing, and criticise them to their faces. My role in the show was to be terrifying, in that superior, Miranda Priestly from *The Devil Wears Prada* way. When you edit *Vogue*, the general assumption is that you are going to be frightening and superior, so you have to work very hard to prove that you're not. It's exhausting. I would at times have my own management tell me that so-and-so was frightened of me, and when I would reply, 'Why, what did I do?' they'd say: 'Nothing, they're just scared of you.' I was accused of being terrifying by people I hadn't actually met. It's a tedious and somewhat ludicrous consequence of the job. But that was the persona they wanted me to play.

As it turned out, I didn't need to play it up much: the poor ANTM girls were absolutely scared stiff when they arrived, so I just went with it and did my *Prime Of Miss Jean Brodie* routine. When the twelve finalists filed into my office, one girl, Alice Burdeau, stood out immediately. She was five-foot eleven, skinny and pale, with large, slightly melancholy eyes and long, thick red hair. She already looked like an off duty model. I could just see her backstage in Paris, reading a book, wearing motorcycle boots and being made up for a runway show. She was the real deal, I could see it. She looked international; there was something cool about her.

I joined the ANTM panel for two more segments after that, which was tons of fun, with designer Alex Perry, model agent Priscilla Leighton Clark, personality Charlotte Dawson, model 'mentor' Jonathan Pease and photographer Jez Smith. Gorgeous Jodhi Meares was hosting, and the atmosphere on set was very warm and good spirited. I was not involved in the filming of most of the stunts and shoots, but was called in on the panel to judge how they appeared in photographs. I swiftly realised the show was also raising my profile, because I kept getting stopped by eager young girls when I went shopping.

There was some negative coverage regarding Alice being underweight, but I knew that—rightly or wrongly—even if she was, her protruding clavicles were just the ticket for the world of high fashion. Alice won easily, purely because of her beauty. She didn't have a great deal of energy, and was not the best model in the world when it came to striking a pose, but when the moment is captured she looks great. Full stop. All the judges were in total agreement, as were the viewers. We immediately set up her shoot, based around long, flowing eveningwear, with photographer Troyt Coburn.

The resultant images were very beautiful and we quickly saw that one of the shots was cover material. She was seated, staring down the barrel of the camera, and she looked serene and self-assured. Although we were not contractually obliged to run a cover, it made sense to me to do so. Sales on that issue lifted 13 per cent. As I had hoped, our involvement in the show had helped us to reach a new readership.

Alice went on to work internationally, hitting the runways for all the big designers in New York, Milan and Paris, such as Marc Jacobs, Jil Sander, Lanvin and Dolce & Gabbana. She was the most credible winner the ANTM franchise had ever had—globally. I always felt a tinge of pride when she swept past me at subsequent shows. The whole association had been win/win, and Alice was a legitimate star who still models regularly five years on.

The experience of the next series, number four, however was very different. When I was first introduced to the contestants, I struggled to find a girl who I thought had true potential. They were all pretty, but there wasn't a standout. One girl, Sam, had the best legs I've ever seen, but apart from that there wasn't one girl I would have considered booking for *Vogue*. It struck home that discovering someone like Alice was a miracle.

The first segment I filmed involved the girls being given five minutes to rush into a room full of clothes, put together an outfit, and then place themselves in front of a panel while I and designer Fernando Frisoni appraised and/or criticised them. Perhaps I was taking it a bit too seriously, because I was stressed and irritable and really needed to get back to the office, but it struck me that the whole exercise wasn't fair. The clothes provided were frankly horrible, and the girls weren't given enough time to think, let alone style themselves. It was an impossible task, and it felt like we were belittling them. Charlotte Dawson was brilliant in the series at playing the cranky mentor with the heart of gold, but I was struggling with the stupidity of the exercises.

The second part of the episode, filmed on the same day, involved magazine covers where the girls had to pick a card with the name of a supermodel on it and 'Match the Supermodel to the Cover'. It was imbecilic.

I felt a similar sense of injustice when a bad photograph was taken of a girl and she was then criticised for 'not bringing it to the camera', when in fact the photographer should have been blamed for their crappy shot. Every element on a shoot counts: the photographer, hair, makeup, styling. The model is one component and certainly can't be singled out for the amateurism of others. Also, as a mother and as a professional, I wasn't comfortable telling a young, hopeful girl that she had a huge, huge future as a successful model ahead of her when I knew full well she didn't.

Over the years, I have had many young women approach me, sending photos to the office, wanting to become models. I would always refer them to reputable model agencies, as it requires a professional to deal with the often unrealisitic expectations of young girls, and their families. Only very few girls, around the world, have what it takes to appear in *Vogue*. A genetic one in a million.

The voting process on ANTM is indeed democratic, and the audience cast the deciding vote at the season finale. The eventual winner, Demelza, had been accused of bullying one of the other girls during the series, but she won the car anyway. I did not agree with the decision. I went backstage after the finale to find the girl she had purportedly bullied in hysterics and had to try to console her.

For weeks afterwards I was bombarded with emails from furious readers, threatening to cancel their subscriptions. Even though I had voted for the other finalist, it appeared that the viewers were incensed that *Vogue* was even on the panel. Our online chat room, the *Vogue* Forum, went into meltdown. The whole situation had, all of a sudden, become quite problematic, and very 'off-brand' for us.

A side effect of being the editor of *Vogue* is that the public expect you to also set a moral benchmark, which is slightly bizarre when you think about it. I mean, it's a fashion magazine full of shoes and bags. But the brand values of *Vogue* represent manners, respect and integrity, and so the backlash was fierce. The public consensus was that *Vogue* had made the decision, which was entirely erroneous. I realised after that experience that the power of the *Vogue* masthead meant that we had to be in total control of the outcome, or we risked losing credibility. ANTM and *Vogue* agreed to part company thereafter.

Demelza was duly given her eight pages as pledged, but no cover, which the media whipped up and interpreted as a snub by me, but in fact we were under no obligation to run one. ANTM aligned with *Harper's Bazaar* after that and they did unearth some credible models such as Montana Cox and Amanda Ware. We continued to shoot Alice for *Vogue* over the next few years. She was, as it turned out, that one in a million.

15

GOLDEN YEARS

Vogue Australia was due to celebrate its fiftieth anniversary in 2009, and it struck me that I was the last one left in the building who had long-standing experience and knowledge of the history of *Vogue*. I was the only person there with more than two decades of corporate or cultural memory. I recruited my dear friend, author Lee Tulloch, to coedit a book with me to record this important milestone, as she had an astute understanding and appreciation for the brand. HarperCollins were engaged as publishers and we set to work, with the help of erstwhile editorial coordinator Kimberley Walsh.

One would expect there to be a gleaming archive of painstakingly sorted *Vogue* material, but in fact all that exists are some leather-bound copies of the magazines that have to be taken out of the stacks and photocopied. No photographic library of all the shoots was ever kept, and any film that did remain was thrown willy-nilly into boxes and stored in a shed on the FPC premises. Poor Kimberley spent days cautiously picking through water-damaged and possibly rat-infested piles of unidentified film to salvage any original material whatsoever. The whole endeavour was a gruelling exercise, but Lee, Kimberley and I all shared a passion for having the history of the magazine recorded, both for ourselves and for posterity. I felt that *Vogue* was changing, especially with the departure of many of the Condé Nast stalwarts. It became terribly important for Lee and I to capture what it had been.

We worked laboriously to finish on deadline, with Lee completing an enormous amount of research and stellar writing within a miraculous timeframe. It was a six-month slog, and probably the most exacting editing job I ever had. We had to turn five decades of, quite frankly, patchy material, into something glossy, concise and impactful. When the first advance copy of the book *In Vogue: 50 Years of Australian Style* arrived on my desk, fresh from the printers, Kimberley and I burst into tears, overcome with a sense of achievement and relief. Lee and I packed all the photocopies of the magazines into a box, and I left it in the stockroom as a time capsule for the next editor of *Vogue Australia*.

Once the book was finished, we had to get cracking on the anniversary issue of the magazine itself. During a brainstorming meeting with all the *Vogue* editorial staff, the then art director Ella Munro put forward a brilliant cover idea.

I had already suggested the idea of featuring Cate Blanchett. I have always thought her beauty, talent and intelligence combined to make her the quintessential *Vogue* covergirl. The big debate would be how we approached it: which photographer, how she would be dressed, and the feeling we wanted to portray for such an important milestone issue.

Ella had gathered together a series of portraits by renowned English fashion illustrator David Downton. 'I thought it would be lovely to have an illustrated cover,' she proposed. 'It would show a beautiful sense of continuity, pulling the history of fashion illustration through to the present day by featuring a contemporary celebrity, in contemporary fashion.' I got goosebumps. I loved the idea. It was redolent of the past, yet modern in its use of a current actress. As the discussion progressed we decided we would create four different covers, including one deluxe version with a hand-illustrated *Vogue* masthead, which would be sold in its own gold box at a slightly higher price.

The concept was there. Now we had to make it happen.

* * *

Cate was in London, filming the movie *Robin Hood*, co-starring my favourite Russell Crowe. David Downton also lived outside of London and, once contacted, eagerly agreed to the commission. I telephoned Cate's agent in LA, Lisa Kasteler of WKT, to pitch the idea. In the tradition of all celebrity agents, Lisa is tough. If she's not on board it's not going to happen, full stop. I went into my spiel about what we envisaged, and how Cate was my one and only choice for the cover, which was true. I explained the idea of the illustrations and how Cate could nominate the designers she would like to wear, and we would do an old-fashioned portrait sitting with David, with full hair and make-up. Lisa was quiet on the other end of the line for what seemed like an eternity, when finally she replied: 'I think that's a wonderful idea.' Coming from Lisa Kasteler, I knew we were on a winner.

The sitting was arranged to take place at The Dorchester Hotel. Lisa would be attending so it was crucial that I be there to make sure proceedings flowed smoothly and we achieved the four covers we needed. I was also doubling as the stylist.

Lisa and I met for breakfast and stationed ourselves in the hotel's grand lobby, waiting for Cate's arrival. She had a day off from her shooting schedule and was dropping her children to school first. She swept in briskly, with total professionalism as usual, and we took the lift to the suite we had booked for the day.

It's something I love about Cate; she's always ready to get straight to work. She had chosen to wear four designers: Balenciaga, Alexander McQueen, Giorgio Armani and Australian Martin Grant. They were very lavish, very formal pieces, as Cate seems to fall into a shoot more comfortably if there is a sense of theatre about the clothes.

I had also organised for some very special and hugely expensive Tiffany jewels, necklaces and rings to be flown in, and they were there with their own bodyguard. Cate and I did the prerequisite try-on of all the clothes I had hanging in the dressing room until we settled on what she felt best in. I mentioned that I could hardly wait to see her in the upcoming Sydney Theatre Company production of *A Streetcar Named Desire*. 'Oh no, don't put so much pressure on me,' Cate laughed. I was stunned to hear that even someone with the formidable talent of Cate Blanchett possessed an element of self-doubt. I voiced my surprise. 'I often think I am Blanche DuBois,' I confessed, admitting my penchant for complicated Tennessee Williams heroines. 'You know, there's a little bit of Blanche in all of us,' Cate replied.

The process of the sitting was unusual in that the team, which included the amazing hairstylist Sam McKnight and makeup artist Dotti, would get Cate ready in full hair, makeup, clothes and accessories, and present her to David. Afterwards, we retired to my room, leaving them alone to capture the moment. Normally a shoot will have at least ten people on set, but David's work required intimacy, and a personal connection to his subject. Each sketch took approximately half an hour, after which David would summon us back to the suite to start over again. These were the initial drawings, which he would later work on and perfect to produce the final images. It felt rather old-school and marvellous. It was also, for me as an editor, a joy to have such a controllable process—we could execute a headshot, a full length, a three-quarter length, whatever we desired, in the knowledge that every one of them would work. We could make them work. You cannot do that with film. You either get the shot, or you don't. But with illustration, we could embellish, tweak, play. I felt—well I hoped—the reader would see them as a present. They were exquisite enough to be framed.

* * *

Writing the book was one thing; producing the fiftieth anniversary issue was another. But nothing was more stressful than planning the fiftieth anniversary party. Deciding who should be on the guest list was exhausting and highly political, as we strove to create a delicate balance of past and present, and of industry, clients and party people. News Magazines events director Fiona Westall managed to secure the sound stage at Fox Studios, in Sydney's Moore Park, a venue that had never previously been used for a party. The building itself had the appropriate grandeur, with a flight of stone steps leading to the entrance doors. Add searchlights and you had dazzling, Hollywood-style glamour. Rizer Productions built a clever and sumptuous venue within a venue, creating an 'intimate' feel for what was to be around 900 guests.

Despite a global financial crisis, gloomy publishing predictions and a not insignificant cost, News Limited came to the party, so to speak. There were numerous requests on my party wish list: 'Never-ending magnums of ice-cold Moët & Chandon', 'an oyster bar serving dirty martinis' and 'indoor trees', but my greatest wish was that Cate Blanchett be there to launch our fabulous covers. As the stress (and the costs) were mounting exponentially in the weeks leading up to the night, I received a phone call from Cate's local agent. Her client was unfortunately going to have to decline the party, as she was right in the middle of rehearsals for *Streetcar*.

I was driving somewhere in Botany, on my way to work, when I got the news. I pulled the car over and burst into tears. (When I look back I spent a great deal of time in the back streets of Alexandria trying to sort out problems.) It's difficult to get celebrities to events these days. It's all marketing and business. Unless they are promoting something for themselves they're not interested. In many cases, you have to pay them. It's a minefield of tedious negotiations. I find the idea of paying someone to go to a party odious. Cate never demands money, and I accepted that she was in rehearsal.

I felt miserable about it for a couple of days and then I decided to make one more last ditch attempt. It's part of my career philosophy—it won't hurt to ask. I think my Scottish grandmother taught me that, although her version was: 'If you don't ask, you won't git.'

I called Lisa Kasteler and was completely transparent. 'Lisa, I know how it all works, believe me. I understand that Cate is busy. But this means so much to me, not in order to get publicity for *Vogue* in particular, but to me personally. I'm so proud of this project.'

Lisa said 'Leave it with me,' and hung up.

Cate confirmed her attendance a few days later. Honesty is the best policy. A Hollywood agent, just like a gossip columnist, can spot a scam a mile away. Lisa and Cate were simply being gracious.

I had been rehearsing my speech for about, oh, six months, lying awake in bed between the hours of 2 a.m. and 4 a.m. It was such a momentous occasion for *Vogue*—and for me—I had to get it right. I wanted to acknowledge everyone who had contributed to *Vogue* over the years, what fifty years in fashion publishing meant, why we were celebrating, everything *Vogue Australia* had achieved. All without sounding like a gushy fool.

The night of the party, I dressed at Lee Tulloch's home beforehand. To avoid the problem of favouring one designer, I chose a black, forties-vintage dress that I had found in Paris for $100. My hair and makeup channelled the fifties, B-grade actress once again, with a lot of backcombing by my date for the evening, trusty hairdresser Bruce Packer, and with help from Kate from Napoleon, who layered on the eyeliner and lipstick with a trowel (at my insistence).

PR supremo Tracy Baker was also working on the event, and instead of a red carpet had installed a long stretch of zebra, flanked down each side by male models in black tie. John Hartigan and I stood and received every guest, as seemed fitting, but unfortunately there was a bottleneck for a period which meant a few of the guests were shivering outside in the chilly night air. Then suddenly, the space was filled. I was standing by the side of the stage, chatting to Joel Edgerton, who was also in rehearsals for *Streetcar*, playing Stanley. I mentioned I was about to go up and speak. 'You don't seem very nervous,' he said. 'Well, I don't think anyone wants me to fail do they?' I said hopefully, and he agreed that was the best way to approach it.

That and two champagnes.

Sandra Hook and John Hartigan both gave short, succinct speeches and then Bernard Leser, the man who was responsible for *Vogue Australia*, delivered my favourite line of the night during his elegant address: 'Do quality work first and the profits will follow.' You won't hear anybody in management say things like that anymore.

Then it was my turn. The audience gave me a cheer, and I felt so buoyed and grateful and happy to be there it seemed to be over in seconds. The event was not to celebrate me as custodian, or to give lofty pronouncements on the power and authority of *Vogue*. It was to celebrate each and every person in the room, who had in some way contributed to the magazine over time. Afterwards, I was led down the steep stairs from the stage by two male models and walked over to stand next to Cate Blanchett, looking splendid in a red Ossie Clark vintage dress. 'Gee, you really know how to deliver a good speech,' she said. This, coming from Cate Blanchett, the world's greatest actress. You could have picked me up off the floor. I'll remember that compliment forever.

A few minutes later the DJ played 'Vogue' by Madonna, and the party ignited. The staff, the entire Australian fashion industry and I hit the dance floor and stayed there until closing.

A week later we held a fiftieth anniversary celebration dinner in Melbourne, which was momentous for the fact that there were three *Vogue Australia* ex-editors present: Sheila Scotter, June McCallum and Nancy Pilcher.

Sheila, who has since sadly passed away, was well into her nineties, so to have all these impressive women in the same room was quite an achievement. Sheila certainly had all her wits about her, but she could be cantankerous to the point of nastiness, so I paired her off with the charming and patient *vogue.com.au* editor Damien Woolnough for the evening. John Hartigan made a surprise appearance during the night, and presented me with the *de rigueur* Tiffany box, containing two Elsa Peretti bangles, to commemorate my ten years as editor of *Vogue*.

The fiftieth anniversary issue, September 2009, was launched: four different covers, one in a limited edition gold box. A few months later I was thrilled to find that the issue was voted one of US *Time* magazine's Top Ten Covers of the Year. We were nominated for Best Magazine at the annual News Limited Awards and I thought we were a shoe-in, but *GQ Australia* won for reasons unknown.

Well, at least the editor of *Time* appreciated what we'd done. As did John Hartigan, who wrote me a lovely congratulatory note. I'm not usually one to pat myself on the back. In fact, I always think I can do better. But for once, I allowed myself to accept the praise.

16

FINAL DEADLINE

In late 2011 Condé Nast International Chairman Jonathan Newhouse proposed that every *Vogue* editor-in-chief should travel to Tokyo to host a very special Fashion's Night Out, a celebration that had been originally instigated in 2009 by Anna Wintour in the US. The general idea was to create a party-like atmosphere for one night in the stores, and it was designed to help stimulate retail by involving designers, models and celebrities. Each *Vogue* editor globally hosts the event in their respective cities, all on the same date in September.

Japan was still reeling from the devastation caused by the recent earthquake and tsunami, and to have all the editors come together to show our support, including Anna, was a landmark event for Condé Nast. Our first task was to assemble in the foyer of the Grand Hyatt hotel, and be ushered into a room to have a group photograph taken.

Seating positions had clearly been worked out beforehand, with Anna front and centre, flanked by Franca Sozzani from *Vogue Italia* and British *Vogue*'s Alexandra Schulman, and Emmanuelle Alt from Paris *Vogue* seated on the floor in front. I was at the back on the left, half obscured by Yolanda Sacristan from *Vogue Spain*. The pecking order was breathtakingly apparent. I had grown used to acknowledging the power and importance of the bigger *Vogue*s, but the emergence of markets such as China, India and Turkey and their commonsense editors had helped to make me feel a little less marginalised.

I had no dealings with Anna Wintour over the years, and on the few occasions we were introduced her sense of froideur was palpable. The deference she commands from people is astonishing to watch. There appears to exist some kind of psychological condition that causes seemingly sane and successful adults to prostrate themselves in her presence. It's not just respect—it's something else. People actually want to be scared witless of her, so she obliges. It's very clever when you think about it. Many times over the years, people, after they had met me would say, 'Oh gee, you're so nice and normal', often I think with a tinge of disappointment, wishing I'd been just a little bit like Anna. I could never really win. I was either expected to be terrifying or snobbish. And I don't consider myself either.

The next afternoon the editors were put into pairs (apart from Anna who was with her daughter Bee) and taken to visit various stores and boutiques around Tokyo. The crowd scenes that erupted around any appearance of Anna were astonishing. I was with Alex Shulman from British *Vogue* and if we saw that Anna was approaching the store we were in, we would beat a hasty path out to avoid being crushed in the mob. It was one of the craziest days in my career.

Earlier in the proceedings the editors and all the visiting designers, including Michael Kors, Christopher Bailey from Burberry and Peter Copping from Nina Ricci, had been herded into a multi-levelled shopping mall, and into a specially erected backstage area. A large board covered in tactical diagrams had been set up, and a Japanese organiser with limited English and a long wooden pointer explained that we were to all file into the mall, and be announced one by one to the waiting crowd. It was like a demented military operation.

I took my place in the queue as we all waited nervously to have our name called. I heard 'Kirstie Clements, *Vogue Australia*', and I emerged into the light to see a flight of dauntingly steep stairs leading to a stage, and the stony face of Anna Wintour waiting at the top, surrounded by hundreds of Japanese shoppers looking down on us all, cheering and waving. It was like being dropped into some bizarre version of the Eurovision Song Contest. Anna launched into a speech by shouting 'Hello Tokyo!' and I thought, maybe I should write a book. You couldn't make this stuff up. One minute you are in a drab office in downtown Sydney being pummelled from every direction and asked to cut costs, reduce staff, increase circulation, improve marketing, innovate artistically, stop the use of skinny models, send an anti-fur message, maintain modern morality, solve the problem of how to monetise new media, meet every client request, and work out what the weather might be next Thursday; the next you are on an international stage being cheered like a contestant in a fashion *X Factor*.

By early 2012 there had been another change of management, and Sandra Hook was no longer the CEO of what was now called NewsLifeMedia rather than News Magazines, a new name to better reflect the digital areas we were moving into. We all waited with some trepidation to discover who her replacement would be and the usual jostling for power began in the middle management ranks.

It's an unfortunate side effect when a company is in transition that you really see people's true colours, as they try to make tactical allegiances through blind panic. Given that this would be yet another boss for me, I was cautiously optimistic. Naively, I anticipated the new arrival would perhaps appreciate my insights and knowledge of the market. I thought I could add value. I knew full well *vogue.com.au* was looking tired and did not reflect the brand, and we were waiting for funds to be approved for a redesign. We had created and launched our first app to promote the December 2011 issue which was well-received, and there were plans in the pipeline for a second. But I wasn't able to see these plans come to fruition. There were forces at work that would soon see me unceremoniously dumped from my position, and almost the entire *Vogue Australia* editorial team summarily dismissed shortly afterwards.

* * *

Being a *Vogue* editor is precarious, as it's a job everybody desires to have, and most people are convinced they could do better. I recall one of my seven CEOs saying to me rather nastily: 'Oh, are you back from Paris again are you? God, there would be thousands of people lined up around the block who would want your job.'

'Yes, there are, I'm well aware of that,' I replied. 'I guess the question is: can they do it?'

It seems no editor of *Vogue* ever chooses to leave of their own accord, so I'm not taking it personally. It was a business decision, intended to make a statement about change. I'm sure some of the other powerful editors will break this unpleasant tradition of being suddenly fired, such as Anna Wintour, Franca Sozzani and Alex Shulman, but when you work for a magazine that is under licence with a constant stream of new managers, your luck, as it were, is eventually going to run out.

However, I do not put my career down to luck. I was mentored, guided and supported by numerous wonderful colleagues. The motivating force for me was never money, or personal glory or fame—quite the opposite. I loathe social climbers and name droppers. I didn't like the spotlight, and I'd run miles to avoid a red carpet photo. That seems so prehistoric in this new era of Instagramming your breakfast tray. Being gossiped about and sniped at by the media was wearisome and could be hurtful, but I learned to cope. I've never Googled myself. That's a definite highway to hell.

A day or so after I was fired, as if losing my livelihood and a career that I loved was not enough, the media section of *The Australian* decided it would be amusing to ridicule me, and the staff, suggesting all we talked about was nail polish and even questioning how we got a magazine out the door every month for thirteen years. That ugly misogyny really upset me. The *Vogue* team were complete professionals; we prided ourselves on that. The reason I was there all along was for the reader. I absolutely loved making a magazine, and I loved working with my team to try and improve and evolve the product every month. I was harder on myself than anybody else would be if I made a mistake, and when you're the editor of *Vogue*, your slip-ups are very public. But throughout it all I was fortunate to share the ups and downs with the most dedicated editorial team, freelancers and clients.

Traditional publishing is under enormous pressure at present, with declining revenues and readership, and decisions are being made, understandably, to radically cut editorial staff and costs and do anything to please the advertiser. But for me, this is perilous. I still believe in the magic.

Despite all the changes I see in the industry I think that now, more than ever, it is important that your work has integrity. The mediums have changed and will change again, but honest, intelligent content is still key. In a publishing environment where revenue streams and profit margins are unclear and content costs are being slashed, the beautiful execution of interesting and original ideas remains crucial whether in print or online. It is what you are selling.

I like to hope that career success comes from wanting to do a great job, not just making short-sighted decisions in order to keep your job. I'm sure that path always exists, and it's the one I'm going to take.

ACKNOWLEDGEMENTS

I would firstly like to thank my publisher at MUP Sally Heath, who contacted me the day that followed my exit from *Vogue*, and who provided quiet and calm counsel throughout the writing of this book. Also thanks to Lorelei Vashti for the final edit and her encouraging words. I'd also like to thank Penelope White and Terri King at MUP for their editorial and marketing advice. For the author photography I would like to thank photographer Max Doyle, Naomi Smith for styling, Bruce Packer for hair and Linda Jeffreys for makeup.

I was fortunate to work alongside so many wonderful colleagues throughout my twenty-five years in the business who have provided inspiration, intellect and humour, all of which helped to make some sense of the madness that is the world of fashion publishing. Heartfelt thanks to Robyn Holt, Nancy Pilcher, Grant Pearce, Tory Collison, Charla Carter, Sally Bell, Karin Upton Baker, Eric Matthews, Stephen Scoble, Sandra Hook, Georgette Johnson, Paul Meany, Leigh Ann

Pow, Kimberley Walsh, Naomi Smith, Natasha Inchley, Damien Woolnough, Meg Gray, Ilona Hamer, Megha Kapoor, Genevra Leek, David Clark, Alex Spring, Jo Constable, Robert Rosen and a long list of incredible talents who worked at *Vogue* during my tenure and from whom I in turn was privileged to learn from.

There were others in the industry who, via our professional relationships, have become invaluable friends and confidantes: Ian Clark, Anthony Kendall, Lisa Ephson, Tim Blanks, Shemi Alovic, Mary Chiew, Sally Pitt, Napoleon Perdis, Julie Otter, Michelle Wivell, Bruce Packer, Natalie Middleton, Tracy Baker and Sener Besim.

To my much loved and dear friends in the 'Coven': Janet Muggivan, Deborah Thomas and Lee Tulloch—we are definitely keeping each other sane. And to Jenny Power, Pascall Fox and Tim Herbert, I appreciate that you both know full well my past sartorial mistakes and have been able to move past them.

To Stephen Fitzgerald, thank you for your incredible generosity for firstly sweeping me off to Paris for inspiration, and then for providing me with two fireplaces, Sebastian, and a cosy retreat which allowed me to write all winter. Also thanks to Nicholas Cole for his advice.

To my family: my mother Gloria for her rock solid belief in me, Mourad for your unquestioning love and support during all my whims and my constant periods of absence, and to my gorgeous sons Joseph and Sam, for becoming even more amazing as you get older.

INDEX